New Indian Cookery

Meera Taneja was born in India and went to school in Sweden, India, Burma and Pakistan – but remembers spending most of her spare time in friends' kitchens, sampling their cuisines. She specialized in cookery while studying home economics in England, and this formal training in English and French cookery, combined with her background of Indian cookery and culture, laid the foundation for her subsequent work. Later, after a spell of working in Japan, she married and settled in Hertfordshire, England.

Meera Taneja spends most of her time communicating her love of Indian food through books, broadcasting, seminars and television; promoting Indian chefs in India and abroad; and developing original recipes to share with her fellow professionals, friends and acquaintances. Among her books are *The Indian Epicure* (1979), *Indian Regional Cookery* (1980) and *Curry Cookbook* (1982). She is currently writing an Indian cookbook for *Good Housekeeping* to be published in 1983.

Meera Taneja

New Indian
Cookery

Fontana Paperbacks

First published in Great Britain by Fontana Paperbacks 1983
Copyright © Meera Taneja 1983
Reprinted 1984

Set in 11 on 12pt Linotron Garamond

Drawings by Arjun Kashyap

Made and printed in Great Britain by
Richard Clay (The Chaucer Press), Bungay, Suffolk

To my daughters
Priya and Preti
and their generation of cooks

Contents

Acknowledgements

In everything we are and everything we do, we inherit the past, learn from it, criticize it, define problems, and propose new solutions. *New Indian Cookery* builds on the classic traditional cookery by challenging many of its orthodoxies, its limited or non-use of some materials, ingredients and cookery processes. It proposes new recipes based on personal experience of experimenting with spices and herbs, and cooking with other cuisines, particularly Chinese, Mexican, English and French. For my development in Indian cookery I owe thanks to my parents, Madan Lal and Satya Khosla, and to my first ever Indian cookbook by Attia Hosain and Sita Pasricha. For exposure to the other cuisines mentioned above, I owe thanks to books by Kenneth Lo, Diana Kennedy, Tom Stobart, Alan Davidson, Elizabeth David and Michael Guerard, and to my cookery teacher at college, Sue Hewitt.

Two people who have lived with the development of the new Indian cookery over the years and have contributed to it are my dearest friends, Asha and Raj Kubba.

Christine Harding did the typing faster than I could put pen to paper and gave up her valuable evenings and weekends willingly without fuss to complete the typescript. My thanks also to Enid 'Erica' Martin, our children's nanny, who uncomplainingly looked after all of us during the writing of this book, and to Helen Fraser, my editor, for sharing faith and confidence in this idea. My thanks also to Arjun Kashyap who did the drawings.

Finally, I thank Neelam Taneja, my husband and critic, for providing the conceptual framework for this book.

Introduction

This book is very different from all other Indian cookbooks: it describes a new way of cooking and serving Indian food. It departs radically from the classic methods and does not contain well-tried favourites such as *tandoori* or *mughlai*, nor any traditional Kashmiri, Bengali or Hyderabadi dishes.

The classic tradition of Indian cookery is well documented. Most of the methods, ingredients and recipes have been around for a very long time, handed down from one generation to another with very few innovations. However, during the last three decades there has been a gradual change taking place in Indian cookery, in response to the demands of modern living, to the availability of materials and processes new to Indian cookery and to a greater exposure to other cuisines. This change builds on the classic tradition but the result is an exciting and distinctive new Indian cuisine. It is this new Indian cuisine that is described in the following chapters and offers a unique and original experience of Indian food.

The recipes described are the result of experiments with the processes, ingredients and structures of dishes. The emphasis is on dishes where the flavour of the main ingredient, whether it be meat, poultry, fish or vegetables, is enhanced by using appropriate herbs and spices, and cooking with the minimum or no extra fat or water, which is contrary to the classic way of cooking Indian food. I have used herbs and spices selectively to add a subtle, distinct flavour, rather than adding a large array of spices for every recipe – as is the custom in the traditional method. The idea is that no more than two to three spices which are complementary to each other and to the main ingredient be used in any one recipe. This not only increases awareness of the taste but also improves the general appearance and colour of the dish. As it is the subtle use of spices that creates the final taste, I consider it a shame to use too many in any one dish: the end product may be delicious, but its spicing becomes a matter for guesswork. My way of cooking clearly breaks away from that concept. I emphasize the use of maybe just one highly aromatic spice in any one dish, so that when the full meal consisting of a number of dishes is created, each has a totally individual taste, texture, colour and aroma to complement the others. For example, chicken cooked in just ground cinnamon and cloves as the main flavouring and colouring spices, and further enhanced by the use of red and green peppers, thin slivers of fresh ginger and red chilli powder: the whole combination is delicious, yet not over-powering in any way. Gentle sautéing of chicken to tenderize it and stir-frying of the peppers to cook them fast to retain their crunchiness further enhances the dish. This is just one example of the way in which I have used spices so that they keep their own flavours.

A complete range of new marinades has been created specifically for this book, again breaking away from the traditional marinades such as lemon juice or yogurt. In the past, fruit juices have very rarely been used as marinades, yet I find fresh orange juice makes a delicious marinade for lamb, as in the recipe for baked lamb chops. Here again, the emphasis is on just one spice – lightly crushed aniseed. Another very interesting marinade is made with clear honey and lemon juice in which the only spice used to enhance their flavour is ajowan, a spice rarely used with meat but to my mind superb in this marinade. The spice resembles the taste of thyme or celery and combines well with honey and lemon. The chicken is marinated in this mixture then baked in a slow oven to acquire a crisply golden glaze from the honey. Such a dish, like all in this book, need not necessarily be served with Indian accompaniments, but would go equally well with refreshing salads and potatoes tossed in spices.

Baking is a virtually unknown means of cooking in traditional Indian cookery, except in the age-old *tandoor*, an large unglazed clay oven introduced to India by the Persians a long time ago. Tandoori cooking is a highly specialized art, now largely restricted to the restaurant trade and to the communal *tandoorwala* in residential areas of Indian cities and towns. Baking Indian food in a conventional gas or electric oven gives it a new dimension, so much so that a complete meal can be cooked in the oven, thus leaving the cook free to enjoy her/his time. With this in mind I have developed a whole range of recipes from baked dals to desserts which form an integral part of this cookery. Imagine a fish starter, a baked dal, a stuffed vegetable, marinated meat or poultry and finally a dessert all baked in the oven at the same time.

Stir-frying is a tradition normally associated with Chinese cuisine. My love for Chinese cookery prompted a desire to create dishes that would be tender and full of flavour but still have a crunchiness about them. Very often I have used the term 'stir-fry', by which I mean fry over high heat, stirring, to seal in the juices and flavours of the ingredients and at the same time tenderize them.

The vegetables used in this book are both the so-called common ones such as cauliflowers, turnips and swede and the more exotic aubergines, peppers, okra etc. It is interesting to note that the vegetables common in the West, where winters are long and summers short, are luxuries in the East where the seasons are the other way round. For all the vegetables I have developed recipes which require little cooking and no additional water.

This leads me to rice, the staple food of more than half the world's population. Rice is such an interesting ingredient and comes in such a variety of colours, textures, aromas and sizes that it is often difficult for the cook to decide which rice to use or how to cook it. Basmati – the extra-long-grained and fine-textured rice – is considered the king of rice. This is not only because of its size but also because of its aroma. No rice is quite like it, and it is this rice that predominates in the recipes here, though this need not stop you using the rice of your choice, be it patna rice, brown rice or any other. Basmati is also best suited for the traditional *pillaus* and *biriyanis* which, you will notice, are absent from my book, to leave room for new

13

tastes and ingredients. Rice dishes such as salmon rice, coriander rice, spinach rice, all lend themselves beautifully to my new way of cooking, and here again the emphasis is on one spice, one flavouring ingredient at a time.

North Indians are mainly wheat-eaters, hence the breads produced in this region are quite numerous. The white loaf has no place in the classic Indian cuisine although commercially produced bread with no taste does exist. Indian breads fall into two sections: the daily chappati or parantha made with wholemeal flour; and breads such as nan which are made with plain flour and often leavened. Although I have not discovered any new ways of preparing Indian bread, I have created new fillings which are truly delicious, for example those made with spicy chicken or soft cheese. These breads, in fact, are substantial enough to be served as a separate course or for a delicious brunch.

I have included a chapter on drinks and chutneys because they are not only used as an accompaniment to the meal but, in the case of chutneys, also used as stuffings and coatings for meat or poultry or vegetables. What could be more delicious than a spicy mint chutney that is stuffed in a leg of lamb, glazed with honey and slowly roasted in the oven, or a coconut chutney stuffed in boiled cauliflower, or fish cooked in a tamarind chutney, or yogurt chutney with thick pork chops which have been marinated and then baked. Although chutneys form part of an Indian meal in their own right, I find their use as ingredients far more exciting.

Normally water or a light yogurt drink is served with an Indian meal, simply because the richly spiced traditional food kills off any other flavours, but in my new Indian cookery, light fruity or dry white wines and red wines form part of the total concept of the meal. Other drinks that have now become famous all over the world are the yogurt-based lassis. To these various flavours can be added, for example roasted cumin or mint, but lassi flavoured with fresh ginger juice has become a favourite.

Serving desserts and puddings after a traditional meal is quite a recent innovation. Most Indian desserts are made of paneer (soft cheese) or of vegetables soaked in syrups. Although India has an abundance of delicious fruits, which are eaten in their natural state, very little use is made of them in cooking. In this book I have created puddings using fruits and, instead of syrups, yogurt-based sauces, so keeping the calories to a minimum. I have also, for the first time, combined paneer with fruits, as in the creation of mango cheesecake which combines homemade paneer with canned mango purée. The desserts are lighter than traditional Indian puddings, and more distinct in their approach and presentation. An appropriate finale to a superb meal.

A few words about the equipment used in this book. Basically the saucepans, frying pans etc. found in any kitchen are suitable to be used, but it is well worth investing in one or two specialized utensils such as a *karahi* and *tava*.

Karahi: Very similar to the Chinese *wok* but heavier. Its unique feature is its ability to distribute heat evenly, due to its deep concave shape. Its shape also means it uses less oil than other deep-frying pans. And food is very easy to turn over because it simply falls off the *karahi*'s sides. You can buy a *karahi* in most Indian shops.

Tava: A heavy, cast-iron griddle similar to a drop-scone griddle. Ideal for making paranthas which require slow shallow frying because the *tava* retains and distributes the heat so well.

Wherever possible I have used modern electrical appliances such as food processors, blenders, choppers and grinders which make life easier. But less sophisticated equipment can always be used instead.

Throughout the book I have referred to oil without listing any particular type. This is done intentionally because the recipes are based on the use of small quantities of fats so I felt that it would be appropriate to leave the choice to the individual. I myself prefer to use corn oil which is a polyunsaturated oil and good for health and not too expensive.

15

A virtually tasteless oil, it blends very happily with whatever is being cooked in it. A selection of popular oils that are used in traditional Indian cookery are also listed in the glossary section in case the reader wishes to experiment with a variety of new tastes and aromas.

Ghee is often mentioned as a medium to use. Although traditional cooking was usually done in ghee, it is very high in saturated fats as it is made out of butter. Therefore I have kept the use of ghee to the minimum, just as a garnish to be poured over a dish at the last minute. Ordinary salted butter is not recommended as the salt and other sediments stick to the bottom of the pan and burn, so ruining the taste of the entire dish. Unsalted butter can be used but is more expensive than homemade clarified butter or ghee as described on page 45.

Traditionally, Indian food is always served as a complete meal in one course, but in my new concept I have separated the meal into a four-, five- or six-course delight to be enjoyed over several hours. Very often I serve a light starter either at the table or with drinks as an appetizer. This can be followed by a soup or salad, then a fish course on its own. Dals that are delicately flavoured form the next course with either chappatis or rice or the stuffed paranthas served with yogurt on their own. Then I serve a meat or poultry dish with a vegetable and yogurt and an accompanying dish of the appropriate rice. Finally comes the dessert where the impact of the meal – its aromas, flavours, colours and textures – is brought to a fitting conclusion. I hope that the suggestions on pages 39–42 will help you plan your menus so that you produce food which tantalizes the palate and makes the meal a memorable experience.

Critics of this book will say this is not the 'true Indian cookery' as this is not the way Indian food is cooked in India and no one in India separates the meal into courses. My reply would be as follows: like any other cultural process, classic Indian cookery must open its doors to new influences, criticism and experiences, otherwise it will become closed and inward-looking. This stage of change has been reached primarily because of Indians' migration to other cultures where they have acquired an awareness of other cuisines. I have been privileged to travel, live and work in countries away from India, and have had the opportunities to learn from other cuisines as well as to experiment with Indian cookery in such a way as to create a new taste in and style of Indian food which builds on and extends the classical boundaries.

The unconscious process of developing *New Indian Cookery* started in my mind nearly eighteen years ago with a desire simply to create something different. Over the years, with gradual modifications of the traditional recipes, emerged a conscious attempt to create a new style. By the late 1970s it became an absolute obsession and it has taken from then until now to give it shape and structure and to share this experience with you.

The guidelines that I have followed in developing the new Indian cookery are described below.

1. Since the world is becoming cholesterol-conscious, create light and delicious dishes, cooking with minimum fat or water, so allowing the meats, poultry and vegetables to cook in their own juices.
2. Select and use herbs and spices in such a manner that not only do they enhance the flavour of the whole dish, but complement other dishes as well.
3. Use new and exciting marinades made from fruit juices, honey and seeds to create new flavours and textures.
4. Use shorter cooking times to retain the crispness and texture of the pulses and vegetables.
5. Extend the range of cooking methods and equipment to include baking and stir-frying, not previously used in Indian cookery.
6. Create definite courses to bring out the best of each dish rather than serving everything at once as is the normal practice. Although there is certain informality in serving everything together, the purpose and central thesis of the *New Indian Cookery* is to enjoy the unique tastes and flavours in complementary modules and extend the experience of the meal for as long as possible.

7. Encourage a greater awareness of some of the nutritious value and taste of forgotten ingredients such as pulses.

The recipes in this book represent the culmination of several years' experimenting within these guidelines, and I would hope that you will add your own innovations after experimenting with my suggestions. Although you do not need a thorough knowledge of classic Indian cookery, a good read of the glossary and basic recipes would be of great help. To conclude, all I can say is that I hope you enjoy the experience of cooking and eating from *New Indian Cookery* as much as I have enjoyed creating and documenting it.

Glossary of Indian Foods

Fruits and Vegetables

Aubergine or egg plant (*Baingan*)
A native plant of India, it is now available all over the world. It comes in various colours, shapes and sizes. The purple, most common aubergine can be round or long, fat or thin, with a soft white flesh and minute seeds inside. Then there are white and green aubergines which are truly delicious. Slightly bitter, nevertheless a delicious vegetable.

Bitter gourd (*Karela*)
It is believed that gourds were the first vegetables used by man. In certain parts of the world, white and yellow pumpkins are also classed as gourds. Although they come in various shapes and sizes, the one used in this book is bright green with a knobbly skin, white flesh and large edible seeds inside. They are extremely bitter, so need to be rubbed with salt and left to marinate for some length of time to extract the bitterness.

Cabbage (*Bandhgobi*)

Cauliflower (*Phoolgobi*)

Cauliflower stalks (*Dandal*)

Carrots (*Gajjar*)

Tender green chickpeas (*Choliya*)
The tender green chickpea plants are harvested long before
they are fully ripe, and the pods are normally sold on the plant.
Excellent for use in salads and with rice.

Courgettes (*Tori*)

Cucumber (*Kheera*)

Dasheen (*Arbi*)
A root vegetable of the yam family. Treat as potatoes, i.e. boil
in their skins, or peel and deep-fry. Their slight sliminess can
be removed by washing in plenty of cold water. Available in
most oriental stores and some supermarkets.

Fenugreek leaves (*Methi*)
Available fresh or dried, these leaves belong to the clover
family. Bitter in taste, the young plants are used in salads, and
the mature plant as a vegetable. The seed is used as a spice.

Guava (*Amrood*)
A delicately flavoured, slightly perfumed, soft fruit with a pale
yellow skin. The inside flesh can either be pale cream or soft
pink. The hard seeds inside the fruit are also edible.

Ladies' fingers (*Okra* or *Bhindi*)
A beautiful green tapering vegetable, hence its name. It
contains small white seeds and, when cut across, the inside is
shaped like a star. Its slight sliminess is reduced by adding

something acidic. Available throughout the year in the UK in oriental shops and some supermarkets.

Lime or lemon (*Nimboo*)

Mango (*Aam*)

Mushrooms (*Khumba*)

Onion (*Piaz*)

Papaya (*Papita*)
A common tropical fruit. The green pear-shaped fruit grows in bunches at the base of the wide leaves. The inside is a vivid orange-pink with bright shiny black seeds. Delicious when sprinkled with lemon juice. Raw papaya is often used as a tenderizer for meat and poultry. Available in most oriental stores and some supermarkets.

Pimentoes or sweet peppers (*Pahari mirch*)

Pomegranate (*Aanar*)
This hard-skinned fruit has a honeycomb structure of seeds surrounded by a juicy pink flesh. Available in most oriental stores and some supermarkets.

Spinach (*Palak*)

Sweet potatoes (*Shakarkandi*)
A member of the potato family which tastes and smells slightly like sweet molasses. Excellent in salads. Available in most oriental stores and some supermarkets.

Tinda (from the marrow family)
Small round slightly hairy green vegetable with white flesh and small edible seeds. Available in most oriental stores and some supermarkets.

Tomatoes (*Tamater*)

Turnip (*Shalgam*)

Herbs

Although a large variety of spices are used in traditional Indian cooking, surprisingly few herbs have gained any importance.

Basil (*Tulsi*)
A sacred herb, worshipped by the Hindus – as by the Romans, who considered it a herb of fertility. It is never used in traditional Indian cooking, which is a great pity. Because of its medicinal properties, it is often brewed with other spices and tea. I have used it in various dishes in this book with delicious results.

Coriander leaves (*Dhania patta* or *Kotmil*)
One of the most ancient herbs, used for cooking and for its medicinal properties. One of the few plants where everything is used, i.e. root, stems, leaves and seeds, the first three as a herb and the seeds as a spice. The thin fan-like leaves at the bottom of the plant are topped by feathery-looking leaves. An excellent herb for garnishing the dish, although people unaccustomed to it sometimes find its high pungency offensive. Definitely worth a try.

Curry leaves (*Curry patta* or *Meetha neem*)
People commonly mistake curry leaves for bay leaves (*tej patta*). Although all these have shiny leaves, there the similarity ends. Curry leaf is thin, highly aromatic and has a distinct 'curry' flavour. It is best to use fresh leaves as dried leaves lose their colour and aroma very fast. Now readily

available in most Indian stores. Delicious when added to lentils, beans and yogurt dishes.

Garlic (*Lasun*)
A difficult ingredient to categorize – is it a herb or a spice? Whatever it is, it is delicious only when used in small quantities because, being highly smelly, it can destroy a dish if too much is used. One of the healthiest herbs to eat on a regular basis, garlic comes in various shades of colour, from white-skinned to pink to purple, but the clove inside is usually creamy white. As different countries grow different varieties, i.e. some with extra-fat cloves, others with very thin cloves, it is up to the individual to find the right balance.

Mint (*Podina*)
One of the most widely used herbs all over the world, although many varieties exist and the flavour varies from country to country. A most refreshing herb which imparts a cooling effect. Excellent with meat, poultry and yogurt dishes.

✦

Nuts, Oils, Flavours and Essences

Almonds (*Badam*)
True Western and Mediterranean almonds are not commonly available in India. Almonds in India usually come from Iran or Afghanistan and are extremely expensive. Smaller nuts called *chirongi* or *cuddapah* nuts are also used in both sweet and savoury traditional cooking.

Cashew nuts (*Caju*)
A native of India, it is now a favourite all over the world. A creamy white kidney-shaped nut that has a very bland taste. Excellent just lightly fried and tossed in salt or used with meat, poultry and salads.

Coconut cream (*Nariyal ki malai*)
Can be bought in solid state in most Indian and West Indian shops. Dissolve with hot water and use as coconut milk.

Coconut milk (*Nariyal ka dudh*)
Made by scraping or grating the white flesh and squeezing it to extract the milk. See page 49.

Groundnut oil (*Moongphali ka tail*)
Groundnuts, or monkey nuts or peanuts, as they are commonly known, are a good source of excellent oil. When purified, the oil is almost tasteless and very light in colour, similar to olive oil, and sometimes used as a substitute for olive oil.

Mango powder (*Aamchoor*)
Unripe green mangoes are peeled and the light green/white flesh cut into strips and dried in the sun. These dried slivers are then either used whole to flavour a dish or ground into a fine powder. Unripe mango is very sour but has a pleasant tang. Excellent when used in salads to give that extra zing to any dish requiring a little acidity.

Mustard oil (*Sarson ka tail*)
A widely used oil in north and east India, both for cooking and as a body oil. Young babies and children are often massaged daily with a little warmed oil. Although slightly smelly and pungent, it lends a delicious flavour to any dish. A dark-coloured oil, it is often heated to smoking point to alleviate the pungent taste and smell.

Pomegranate seeds (*Anardana*)
Although delicious as a fresh fruit where the pulpy seeds are either eaten as a fruit or pressed to extract the juice, it is the dried seeds that are used in cooking. The pulp sticks to the seed and traps all the tangy taste. The seeds are washed, soaked in water, then ground to be used in chutney.

Rose water (*Gulab ka pani*)
Rose water is an essential ingredient in the flavouring of traditional Indian sweets and desserts. Rose petals are packed closely with sugar crystals to form *gulukand* – a rose flavour candy. Rose water is often sprinkled on newly married couples to bless them. A few drops is usually enough to flavour the dish.

Screwpine (*Kewra*)
Although similar to rose essence, screwpine is inferior in quality. The highly scented flowers of the screwpine trees found in the swampy backwaters of Kerala are used to produce the essence. Cheaper than rose water, it makes a good substitute. One to two tablespoons are often needed to flavour a dish.

Sesame oil (*Gingelly* or *Til ka tail*)
One of the most important oil seeds, in its pure state the oil is colourless and odourless and, in fact, tasteless. As it does not go rancid it can be stored for a length of time in hot climates. Used in the manufacture of margarine.

Silver leaf (*Varak*)
Extremely thin sheets of beaten silver (or gold) which are used to decorate or garnish a rich dish. Tiny pellets of silver are placed between sheets of paper, which is encased in a leather pouch. This pouch is then hammered with a heavy metal hammer to flatten the pellets into thin leaves. Can be purchased in specialist shops. Highly prized in the old days for its mineral content.

Tamarind (*Imli*)
A large shady tree that grows wild all over India. The large pods are very sour when unripe and green. The sharpness mellows as the pods mature and become dark brown and sticky. Often sold in oriental shops as a closely packed slab containing the sticky pods, fibres, skin and seeds. This has to

be soaked in warm water to extract the pulp (see page 50). Concentrated tamarind pulp is also available.

❦

Pulses (*Dals*)

Although pulses have always played a very important part in the diet of people from countries such as India, the Middle East and China, the affluent Western countries are only just beginning to wake up to pulses' nutritious value and include them in their diets. So without trying to sound smug and say 'we told you so', the vast majority of Indians thrive on a daily bowl of pulse of some sort. Being high in protein and fibre, they perform a dual role for the efficient functioning of our system. As a large proportion of Indians are vegetarians, pulses provide the essential protein, as well as roughage which is often removed from the more refined foods.

Due to the influx of immigrants to the UK, every kind, colour and size of pulse is readily available and, do let me assure you, are well worth a try. As a majority of them are fairly bland, they can be combined with all sorts of other ingredients, such as meat, poultry, vegetables etc., and of course be converted into a whole variety of dishes, such as rissoles, *kofte* etc., and even milled into fine flours, which make excellent batters.

As there is such a large variety of lentils, beans and dried peas available on the market, my selection for those to be included in the chapter on pulses became even more difficult. Therefore, I have chosen some of the better known and cooked them in different ways with interesting garnishes: I have either boiled the pulse or baked it to the required consistency, then garnished with spices such as ajowan or fenugreek leaves, plain yogurt with curry leaves, fried or roasted desiccated coconut and many other combinations. One special *dal* that has become a favourite is baked *channa dal* with crispy bacon garnish.

Here is just a brief description of the dals that are used in the pulse chapter.

Black Chickpea (*Kale channe*) Belongs to the same family as the white chickpea but is smaller, and brown in colour.

Black gram (*Urad* or *Ma*)

1. WHOLE BLACK GRAM (*Saabat ma or urad*)
A shiny slightly rounded bean which is jet black in colour. A heavier dal than the moong bean, by which I mean it is more difficult to digest, hence is cooked with a variety of digestive spices. The whole bean needs prolonged cooking, at the end of which it becomes very creamy. I prefer to boil the bean so that it just splits and is tender, then toss it in spices.

2. THE SPLIT DAL WITH SKINS (*Urad or Ma dal chilke wali*)
The bean is split into two with the skins still intact. A delicious dal that is first soaked and boiled to a creamy consistency. Ground, it makes a variety of rissoles and dumplings which are used with yogurt in traditional cooking.

3. THE SPLIT DAL WITHOUT SKINS (*Dhuli hui ma or Urad dal*)
This last version is washed to remove the skins and is often combined with channa dal or cooked on its own to a dry consistency. Has a slightly nutty flavour.

Bengal gram (*Channa dal*)
This must not be confused with the yellow split pea. The channa dal is the split chickpea – which is dark brown in colour. Once the skin is removed the bright orange/yellow dal is sweated. A dal high in protein, it is often used as animal fodder especially for horses. The dal is delicious with a slight nutty flavour and combines well with a wide variety of

garnishes. Excellent when baked in the oven. It does need pre-soaking as it is quite a hard dal.

Egyptian lentils (*Saabat masoor*)

1. WHOLE
Various varieties of this dal are used in different parts of the world, but the ones that are most familiar in the West are the pink split ones, used for lentil soup. The whole bean has a dark reddish-brown skin and needs a fairly long cooking time. Excellent for protein, and makes delicious soups.

2. SPLIT
This split orange/pink dal is a very easily digestible dal and takes only a few minutes to cook. Usually cooked to a fairly thin mushy consistency, it is ideal for recuperating patients and the elderly.

Moath
A thin elongated light brown shiny bean, which requires long cooking to get through its tough shell. One of the most delicious beans, which also makes excellent soup. If over-cooked becomes mushy, but that too enhances its flavour.

Moong beans (*Moong*)
Three versions of the moong bean exist in Indian cooking.

1. MOONG BEAN (*Saabat moong*)
A small, slightly oval-shaped bean, bright olive green in colour, one of the most commonly used pulses in India. The green skin being fairly tough, the bean requires prolonged slow cooking (although it can be speeded up in a pressure cooker). A bean with a slightly musky flavour, it is very popular as the sprouted moong or mung bean used in Chinese cookery.

2. SPLIT MOONG BEAN WITH SKINS (*Moong dal chilke wali*)

The moong bean is mechanically split into two halves but with the skin intact on both halves. The bean inside is pale yellow. When soaked, the skin does come away, but when cooking the skin is not discarded. The taste and texture of this pulse is different to that of the whole moong bean, and takes less time to cook.

3. SPLIT WASHED MOONG DAL WITHOUT SKIN (*Dhuli hui moong dal*)

Here, the bean's skin has been completely removed. The pale yellow dal is very easily digested and often given to recovering patients, old people and young children. The split bean is usually soaked and cooked to a mushy or dry consistency, and takes very little time to tenderize.

Red kidney beans (*Rajma*)

A large, beautiful-shaped bean of the most gorgeous maroon colour, widely eaten in north India, Mexico and South America. A tough bean that needs prolonged soaking in order to swell up. After that it still needs to be thoroughly boiled for at least 2–3 hours, or a shorter time in a pressure cooker, until the bean is tender but still retains its shape. The boiled liquid makes an excellent soup.

White chickpeas (*Kabli channe*)

Usually known as Italian chickpeas, they are used widely all over the Middle East and the Mediterranean. They need prolonged soaking before they can be boiled as they are very hard in their dried state. To speed up the boiling a pinch of bicarbonate of soda is sometimes added. Delicious when combined with tomatoes and onions or just cooked dry, tossed in spices.

Spices

Ajowan
In appearance and in taste very similar to celery and thyme seed. As it is closely related to the caraway and cumin family, it is a highly digestive spice. Often the seeds are boiled in a little water, or chewed whole with a few grains of salt to cure mild tummy upsets. Ingredients such as lentils, peas and beans often cause wind in the stomach, so to counteract that symptom a few ajowan seeds are added to the preparation, both as a flavouring and as a preventative. A very popular seed spice in fried snacks. The whole seed keeps well indefinitely. Often sold as carum seeds, carum being its botanical name.

Allspice (*Kabab chini*)
A unique spice that tastes and smells of three aromatic spices all at once. A native of Jamaica, its use has spread all over the world. The berries are picked when still green, then dried in the sun where they turn brown. Until recently it was believed that allspice was a blend of certain spices, which of course it isn't, although it tastes like cloves, cinnamon and nutmeg all rolled into one. As the berries lose their aroma rapidly once ground, it is best to grind only small quantities as required.

Aniseed or fennel seed (*Saunf*)
Small oval-shaped, light green or light brown coloured seeds. The seeds have a very distinct aroma and taste, rather like liquorice. Used in the making of green Chartreuse liqueur and also the famous gripe water. A digestive and antiseptic spice which is used as an after-dinner condiment, i.e. a few seeds are chewed on their own or wrapped in betel leaf (*pan*) to aid digestion. As an antiseptic spice it is often brewed with tea for curing minor ailments such as colds and coughs.

Asafoetida (*Hing*)

A spice virtually unknown in the West, it owes its origins to central Asia, expecially Iran and Afghanistan. The spice has a very interesting flavour when used in minute quantities; large quantities will ruin the flavour of the dish. A very smelly spice, rather like bad garlic (due to the presence of smelly sulphur compounds). It is best to buy ready-ground asafoetida as the resin is extremely hard to grind in an electric home grinder. Usually it is pale yellow or brown in colour. It is advisable to store in airtight container away from other spices.

Bay Leaf (*Tej patta*)

The *tej patta* used in Indian cooking comes from the Cassia tree which also supplies the coarse cassia bark similar to cinnamon in flavour if not in appearance. The bay leaf can be used either fresh or dried. The fresh leaves are slightly bitter and have a strong smell, and are best stored for a few days so that the bitter taste disappears but the flavour still remains. Although the two leaves are not identical, I find bay leaves make a reasonable substitute for the Indian *tej patta*.

Black pepper (*Kali mirch*)

A native of the swampy tropical forests of Kerala in southern India, black pepper is now widely grown in all the tropical forests of monsoon Asia and south east Asia. At first the berries are green but when ripe turn orange-red. It is the green berries that are picked and dried in the sun until dark brown or the familiar black. Once pepper has been ground it soon loses its essential oils and all the flavour, so it is most important to grind black pepper in a pepper mill at the last minute. Good-quality peppercorns should be free of stalk and dust, and crushable between the fingernails. If good-quality pepper is available it is sensible to buy a large quantity as the whole peppercorn will not spoil.

Caraway seeds

Similar in appearance to cumin and belonging to the same family, but with a totally different texture and flavour. Must not be substituted for cumin.

Cardamoms (*Illaichi*)

Natives of India, cardamoms are now also grown in other tropical countries. Two distinct types of cardamom are available, the small green pod ('*chootie*' *illaichi*) and the large dark green ('*badi*' *illaichi*). Both the varieties have very strong and pungent aromas. The small black seeds inside the pods should be shiny and slightly sticky with a white membrane around them. This is the sign of good-quality cardamom. The plant grows wild in the hill jungles of south India, along the ravines and under large leafy trees. The tall stalks bearing the pods sprawl along the ground as they grow from the base of the plant. Harvesting occurs every few weeks because the pods ripen at different times. The ripe pods are dehydrated in hot sheds for 24 hours. then sorted and graded. An expensive and highly aromatic spice, only a few are needed to flavour a dish. The seeds can be used whole or ground. It is a spice which also has medicinal properties; for example, when feeling nauseous, chew one cardamom to relieve that feeling. Often eaten as an after-dinner digestive. Black cardamoms are larger and coarser and only used in the preparation of garam masala or in flavouring a dish – never eaten on its own.

Chillies, green (*Hari mirch*)

Due to the immigrant population in the UK and other Western countries, fresh green chillies have become a common sight in most supermarkets. At their best they are firm and shiny, the colour a bright green. Avoid any that are wilted or slightly off colour, as the seeds inside will have discoloured and become soggy. As there is no way of predicting their fieriness it is advisable to be cautious when trying them out for the first time, as each one varies in strength. Some can be deceptively mild for the first few bites and then suddenly explode in your mouth. The fresh chilli is often used in cooking to impart a fresh taste, as well as being eaten as an accompanying dish in itself. Add a little salt when grinding chillies to prevent them from becoming bitter.

Chillies, red (*Lal mirch*)
Dried chillies come in all sorts of sizes, shapes and colours: anything from yellow, red, orange to almost black. Each type varies in its 'heat'. The most fiery chillies are the tiny bird peppers. Ripe chillies are usually red and when dried are either sold whole or ground coarsely or into a fine powder. In small doses they are quite healthy for apart from being a digestive spice they are also rich in vitamin C. The reason why most cuisines from climatically hot countries use chillies is that chillies have a cooling effect – chilli-hot food makes one perspire, which due to the heat evaporating makes the body feel cooler. After handling chillies of any description it is essential to wash your hands thoroughly as they cause irritation, especially if in contact with the face or eyes. Chillies are easy to grind at home.

Cinnamon (*Dalchini* and *Cassia*)
There are two varieties of bark that pass off as cinnamon. The true cinnamon comes from Sri Lanka, whereas cassia bark is from India. The Sri Lankan cinnamon quills that you can buy in the shops are the paper-thin pieces of bark which are stripped from the trees, dried in the sun and then folded into one another to form quills. Cassia bark is coarser and thicker but to my mind has more pronounced aroma and flavour. Both can be substituted for one another. Ground cinnamon loses its aroma very quickly, so buy in small quantities.

Cloves (*Lavang*)
Another highly prized spice that grows in most tropical rain-drenched forests. The area around the plantations is highly perfumed by the clove trees. Although all parts of the tree are highly aromatic, it is the buds that retain the best aroma and flavour. The unopened flowerbuds are picked when pink, then spread out on mats to dry in the sun or over gentle heat,

where they turn into the reddish-brown colour with which we are familiar. Different regions of the world produce different varieties of cloves – but the best-quality cloves are well formed, plump and free of dust. Very often one comes across the shrivelled dusty variety, which should be avoided. Cloves are a highly antiseptic spice, as everyone who has used some clove oil for a toothache knows. As cloves, like other ground spices, lose their essential oils and flavour rapidly, they should be bought whole and ground when required.

Coriander (*Dhania*)
Despite what many Western herb and spice books say, the whole coriander plant is used in Asian and South Eastern cooking. A native of the Mediterranean, it has gained a very important place in Indian cuisine. No dish is complete without the final garnish of chopped coriander leaves. The plant is easy to grow in any soil and sprouts in about three weeks. The fan-like leaves emit a delicious aroma when crushed or chopped. It is important to remember that the seeds have a smell and taste totally different from that of the leaves. The dried seeds are treated as a spice and the best aroma is emitted when they are lightly roasted before grinding. Ground coriander seed is an important thickening agent in traditional Indian cooking, and is the basic ingredient of commercially produced curry powder.

Cumin (*Zeera* or *Jeera*)
An essential ingredient in Indian cooking. A highly aromatic spice that is used whole or when ground into a fine powder, as a flavouring and thickening agent. The seeds when dry-roasted and ground emit a delicious aroma and taste. This is often used to flavour drinks and snacks containing yogurt. There are two varieties of cumin: white cumin (*sufaid zeera*), an elongated seed which is light brown or off-white in colour and has very definite segments; and black cumin (*kala zeera*), not to be confused with nigella seeds (*kalonji*), which is much thinner, without a definite shape, has a stronger and more

pungent flavour, and is more expensive than the white variety.

Fenugreek seeds (*Methi ke dane* or *Methre*)
A mustard-yellow, rectangular-shaped seed that is extremely bitter. It is best to roast it to a dark brown colour so that the bitterness disappears. The leaves of the plant, although bitter, are used as a vegetable, and the young leaves are often used in salads.

Ginger (*Adrak* or *Soanth*)
Ginger is considered to be one of the oldest spices, famed not only for its invaluable contribution to cooking but also to medicine. It is a 'spicy' spice, which when dried becomes even stronger so should be used with discretion. Fresh ginger, which is now available almost everywhere, is crisp and tender. The older the ginger, the more fibrous it will become, but can still be used. An excellent spice to use for giving that extra zing to any dish. It is best to scrape the skin rather than peel it, because of its irregular shape and also because of its essential oils that are trapped under the skin. Keeps well in a cool place. Dried ginger powder loses its flavour very quickly so buy in small quantities.

Mustard seeds (*Rai* or *Sarson*)
Black, brown or white mustard seeds are available in most shops. Although it is quite difficult to distinguish between black or brown mustard seed, they are a good substitute for each other. The brown variety is usually used in Indian cookery and is less pungent than its black cousin. The pungency of mustard is due to the essential oil that is not present in the ripe seed or in the powder, but forms when the seed is fried in oil or when the crushed seed is mixed with water. Delicious as a final flavouring in many lentil dishes.

Nigella seeds (*Kalonji*)
A spice that is often mistakenly referred to as *kala zeera*, with which it has nothing in common. They are also often sold as

wild onion seeds, which is also a mistake. Nigella seeds are small hard triangular black seeds, slightly peppery in taste and mildly aromatic. When fried in hot oil they emit their true aroma. Worth a try.

Poppy seeds (*Khus khus*)
A large variety of poppy plants are grown all over the world. In India the opium poppy flower is cultivated and the seeds are a creamy colour with a nutty flavour. Unlike in the West, where poppy seeds are mainly used in desserts and puddings, they are commonly used in savoury meat dishes in India, both as a flavouring and as a thickening agent.

Rock salt (*Kala namak*)
Commonly found in deep underground cave deposits of dried-up seas. Because of its sulphur deposits, has a very distinctive smell and flavour. It is mainly used in salads and yogurt preparations, and is thought to have medicinal properties. Refined rock salt has a different taste altogether.

Saffron (*Kesar* or *Zaffron*)
A spice that has been in existence long before records were kept. The most expensive spice, hence highly adulterated. The saffron crocus is supposed to have come from Greece and Asia Minor but has been cultivated in various parts of the world, even as far north as Saffron Walden in Suffolk. Between 75,000 and 250,000 saffron crocus flowers are required to produce one pound of saffron. A highly aromatic spice which, when infused in warm water or milk, gives off a delicate yellow/ orange colour. A small pinch consisting of a few stamens are enough to flavour and colour a fair amount of rice or any other dish.

Sesame seeds (*Til* or *Gingelly*)
A native of India, this delicate creamy-coloured seed with a mild nutty flavour is an important source of oil widely used in Indian and Chinese cookery. In the West the oil is often used in the manufacture of margarine. The seeds, being naturally

oily, become very crisp on frying or roasting, hence make an excellent coating material.

Turmeric (*Haldi*)
A widely used spice in Indian cooking, which gives the traditional cooking its distinct rusty colour. A highly digestive and preservative spice that has many medicinal uses as well. It is the root that provides the spice, which, when dried, is ground into a fine spice. Often difficult to grind at home. As it is a cheap spice it is best to buy ready-ground as very little adulteration takes place. One important fact to remember is that as it has a strong dye, so too much of it in any dish will ruin the flavour and turn it bitter. Must never, never be substituted for saffron, as that is asking for disaster.

Indian Names and Cookery Terms

Ande Eggs
Atta Wholemeal flour
Badam Almonds
Bharve Stuffed
Bhoona (Bhooni)
    Dry-roasted or well fried
Chawal Rice
Chilka Skin
Dahi Yogurt
Dudh Milk
Dum Steamed
Gosht Meat
Hare Green
Imli Tamarind
Jaggery Molasses
Keema Minced meat
Khata Sour
Khurmani Apricots
Kishmish Raisins
Kofte Meat or vegetable balls
Maans Meat
Machchi Fish
Malai Coagulated milk
Masala Spices

Masalewale Cooked dry
    with herbs and spices
Moongphali Peanuts
Murghi Chicken
Namak Salt
Namkeen Salty
Paneer Cheese
Pakora Fritters
Phal Fruit
Raan Leg of lamb or mutton
Roti Bread
Saabat Whole
Sabji Vegetables
Sada (sade) Plain
Sufaid White
Sukhe Dry
Tarka (vaghar or *bhaghar)*
    Ghee or oil is heated,
    spices added to it and this
    is poured over the
    prepared dish, often as a
    garnish
Varak Silver leaf
Yakhni Stock

Menu Suggestions

The concept of serving traditional Indian meals in different courses is a very recent innovation. Even so the meal is broken into only two or three main courses. The first course may consist of soup, the main course of a whole selection of dishes such as dal, vegetables, meat or poultry, fish, rice, bread, yogurt, chutney and pickles and salads, all served at the same time. The final course would contain a sweet of some sort, like *kulfi* (Indian creamy ice cream) or fruit or one of the syrupy sweets. I have often felt it a tremendous shame that such a delicious array of dishes are all served together, so much so that the eater has very little awareness of the various tastes, flavours and aromas that his senses are confronted with. As so many different and aromatic spices are used in the course of the meal, it is even more important to separate the food, so that each dish is enjoyed to the utmost and relished.

The menu suggestions in this chapter are a guideline on how different tastes, textures, colours and aromas can be combined together into a highly successful meal. My concept of a contemporary formal dinner party is to break it up into five to six courses so that each taste, each smell, each experience is savoured to the very last mouthful. The whole idea is not to speed up the delightful experience of all these exotic dishes so that what the host/hostess has taken hours to prepare, the guest does not devour in minutes. What could be nicer than a beautifully set table with candles, flowers etc., and then one delightful dish followed by another to be enjoyed by everyone.

Although most of the dishes can be prepared well in advance, it is important to remember that the final touches like hot *tarka*, various herbs and spices should only be added at the very last minute before serving, so that they retain their crispness, flavours and general fresh appearance. Nothing could be more disastrous than a garnish that has been sprinkled on hours beforehand, then the dish warmed up and served. That is a sure way of killing off any sense of excitement at the thought of eating an exquisite meal.

The recipes in this new style of Indian food are totally self-contained, therefore they can either be served as a separate course or as part of the main meal. For example, the yogurts in the yogurt chapter make an excellent course on their own or served as an accompaniment to a dal or meat or poultry dish. Similarly the vegetables can either be served on their own with rice or a plain chappati or parantha, or with the main course consisting of meat or poultry and so on. I am sure that once you have tested and tried the recipes you will soon be able to mix and match your own favourites. The menus given here are just a guideline to help you along until you are accustomed to my way of cooking and presenting food.

Breakfast or Brunch
Chicken paranthas
Plain yogurt
Ginger lassi

Lunch
First Course
Moath bean soup

Main course
Spiced eggs
Lemon rice
Crispy okra in yogurt

Dessert
Avocado cream

Lunch
First course
Chickpea salad

Fish course
Spicy baked prawns

Main course
Meat with spinach
Chappatis
Roasted aubergines in
    yogurt

Dessert
Guava baskets

40

Lunch for Vegetarians
First course
Mushrooms stuffed with soft
   cheese

Main course
Spicy black chickpeas with
   spinach
Whole stuffed cabbage
Chappatis
Crisp ginger in yogurt

Dessert
Mango boats

Dinner
First course
Sweet and sour prawns in
   grapefruit

Salad course
Smoked salad

Third course
Channa dal with bacon tarka
Plain parantha

Main course
Green herb chicken
Large tomatoes stuffed with
   corn
Coriander rice
Spiced liver in yogurt

Dessert
Frozen mango yogurt

Dinner
First course
Chicken with almonds –
   with drinks

Second course
Whole Egyptian lentils with
   fried coconuts
Nan

Third course
Fish wrapped in wine leaves

Fourth course
Smoked salad

Main course
Leg of lamb stuffed with
   spicy mint sauce
Corn rice
Cauliflower in tomato and
   spices
Crisp ginger in yogurt

Dessert
Gambles banana jaggery

Dinner for Vegetarians
First course
Sweet potato and almond
   salad

Second course
Split moong dal with mint
Garlic rice
Spinach in yogurt

Main course
Stuffed whole cauliflower
Roasted red and green
  peppers
Soft cheese paranthas

Dessert
Fresh fruit in yogurt sauce

As I mentioned earlier, these are mere suggestions for you to try, but the main idea is to section off the meal so the whole experience is more memorable.

Basic Recipes

There are a handful of basic recipes that crop up every now and then throughout the book, and I have listed them in this separate chapter so that quick reference can be made. These are just the guidelines and left to the individual to experiment with.

❧

Soft Cheese
Paneer

A very old and traditional way of making cheese, which is both easy and quick as it does not require any prolonged maturing. Ideal for instant vegetarian dishes on those emergencies when the fridge is empty of vegetables, and for instant salads, cheesecakes and puddings, or to top a crisp bread. Various souring agents can be used to separate the cheese and whey, e.g. lemon juice, vinegar, acetic acid etc. If using lemon juice it is best to squeeze more than required as the strength of each lemon is different from the other. Bottled lemon juice is quite adequate for this purpose.

1 litre/1³/₄ pints milk
2 tablespoons (approx.) lemon juice, strained
Clean piece of muslin for straining

1. Pour the milk into a medium-sized saucepan and slowly bring it to the boil.

2. As soon as the milk reaches boiling point, remove from heat and add the strained lemon juice, enough to curdle the milk immediately.
3. Stir the milk with a metal spoon then leave it alone for about 5 minutes so that all the curdled milk has time to rise to the surface.
4. Drape the muslin over a large sieve. Pour the curdled mixture into it and strain. (Reserve the whey for another dish.) Securely tie up the ends of the muslin and hang it over the sink. (I find it most convenient to hook it over the sink tap.)
5. Leave it hanging for 20–30 minutes. Then if the paneer is to be cut into cubes or other shapes, flatten it in the piece of muslin into a firm cake. Wrap the muslin over it and place a heavy object on top (a full kettle does the trick).
6. This will further remove any excess moisture so that the paneer fries without spluttering too much.

Note: If vinegar is being used then use the same amount as lemon juice. But if acetic acid is used then just a small pinch is plenty.

Clarified Butter
Ghee

Like yogurt, butter is an ancient method of preserving milk, and if the butter is clarified, it will keep for a long time without going rancid. It is this clarified butter that is *ghee*, a commodity highly prized – and priced – in Indian cooking. Although butter can be bought in shops in most countries of the world, homemade butter has a unique taste and aroma which is difficult to achieve in commercially produced butter. One of the delights for me when visiting my mother in India, apart from meeting her, is to taste some of her homemade butter and ghee.

To make butter
Full cream milk is brought to the boil and then left to get cold, when all the coagulated thick layer of cream settles on the top. Collect this coagulated milk for a few days and let the cream become a little sour. If you are lucky enough to have a wooden churn, well and good, otherwise place the cream in a food processor and switch on. The cream will soon start to solidify. At this point add some ice-cold water and churn for another few seconds. The butter will soon stick together. Remove from the ice-cold water and keep in the refrigerator. This is the most delicious butter I have tasted.

To make ghee from homemade or bought butter
Place the butter in a heavy-based saucepan over a low flame. Once the butter has melted it will soon start to simmer gently – but do not boil. All the froth will rise to the top and the sediment, like salt, will settle at the bottom. Keep the pan on the fire until the froth settles down and the sediment at the bottom begins to discolour. Carefully, without disturbing the sediment, strain the oily ghee through a piece of muslin. Allow the ghee to cool before storing in a glass or plastic jar. (Don't do what I once did – strained the ghee through a nylon strainer into a thin plastic jar, both of which, to my disgust and shock, melted, and I was left to mop up a flood of ghee.)

As ghee is easy and quite cheap to make at home, it is sensible to keep some handy in the fridge. Ready-made pure ghee is extremely expensive, although you can now buy vegetable ghee; this is not as good as the real thing, but not a bad substitute. Apart from imparting a delicious taste, ghee also has a much higher flash-point than oil, hence is ideal, if expensive, for frying.

Yogurt
Dahi

I often wonder what would have happened if yogurt hadn't been discovered. Imagine how dull Asian cuisine would have been. Yogurt has existed since long before records were kept, and was probably discovered by pure accident. Various theories have been advanced on how yogurt was first created and I am sure each country of the Middle East and Asia can lay claim to its discovery. But the popular story is that once a nomad by mistake poured some milk instead of water into a leather bag and set out on his journey. The heat of the sun and the bacteria in the bag combined to curdle the milk and transform it into yogurt. Imagine the nomad's shock and surprise when he opened the bag to quench his thirst. At first apprehensive to taste, he later decided to take his life in his hands and tasted the set milk. To his immense relief and astonishment, he found that it tasted pleasant and that he had no ill effects, so, fortunately for the rest of mankind, yogurt was discovered. It was soon realized that, apart from its smooth texture and pleasant taste, yogurt was also a superior way of preserving milk.

Yogurt was introduced to the West as recently as the sixteenth century, but its peak in popularity has been reached only during the last fifteen to twenty years, when more importance has been given to health foods. Nowadays many electric gadgets are available to help it to set, but I find there is hardly any need to spend a lot of money buying fancy gadgets when a perfectly solid yogurt can be set in a thick pottery bowl with a lid or in a plastic wide-necked vacuum flask. In fact, any container that will retain the heat is quite adequate. Although the vacuum flask doesn't need to be kept warm, it is advisable to wrap other types of container in an old blanket or cover with a tea cosy and keep in a warm place where it can be undisturbed for up to 6–8 hours. I find the

46

airing cupboard an ideal place. So to make yogurt, all you need to do is buy a small carton of natural set yogurt (there are some brands that do not set so you will have to experiment) and some milk and proceed.

600ml/1 pint milk
2 heaped teaspoons natural yogurt

1. Pour the milk into a saucepan and bring to the boil. Remove from the heat and allow to cool to just above blood heat. (Dip a clean finger into the milk to test the temperature – it should not feel too hot or too cold, just comfortable.)
2. Add the shop-bought yogurt and whisk it in really well.
3. Cover with a lid, wrap in a blanket or any other thick material, put in a warm place and leave to set undisturbed for about 6–8 hours. Use as necessary.

Note: It is important not to move the yogurt during setting as it will not set. Sometimes if too much yogurt has been added or left to set for too long a certain amount of water is released. Do not throw the yogurt away, just mix the water in or carefully drain it away.

❧

Garam Masala, a blend of warmth-giving spices

Although a wide range of spices are used in Indian cookery, a special blend of them holds a unique place in the hierarchy of these delicious aromatic little seeds. They are the reason why so many wars were fought, history changed, empires built and crumbled – for the search to the spice route to India and the spice islands. Cloves, cinnamon, cardamoms, black pepper and bay leaf are the basic spices that go into making garam masala, and are also the spices that are known as 'hot spices'

– 'garam' meaning hot, 'masala' meaning mixture. The feeling from these spices is of warmth rather than the fiery heat of, say, chillies. Almost every region of India has its own recipe for garam masala, but the most simple and basic one is this.

2 tablespoons whole black peppercorns	2 tablespoons cloves
2 tablespoons cumin seeds	16 green cardamoms
2 5cm/2-inch sticks of cinnamon	4 bay leaves

Grind these spices to a fine powder and store in an airtight jar.

❦

Coconut Milk
Nariyal ka Dudh

A delicious and creamy fruit that is widely used in southern and western Indian cookery. A most versatile fruit and plant, no part of which is wasted: the tree is used for firewood; the leaves dried and used for matting; the outer husk of the coconut for making rope; the shell for cooking and making ornamental objects; the milky white flesh for eating and for obtaining coconut milk when fresh and oil when dried; last of all the water becomes a refreshing drink straight out of the coconut. In countries such as Britain where coconut has to be imported it is very rare to find a green unripe coconut which contains plenty of water for drinking, but for coconut milk it is the fully ripened fruit that we need. Most people shake the coconut to find out how much liquid it contains, and it is this murky liquid that is often mistaken for coconut milk; it is in fact the coconut water. Coconut milk is obtained by this method.

1. Grate or scrape the fresh coconut flesh. (As it is fairly hard, be careful not to grate your fingers as well.)
2. Squeeze the grated flesh to obtain the first thick batch of coconut milk.
3. Pour some hot water on to the coconut pulp and leave to soak for 10 minutes then squeeze this to obtain the first thin batch of coconut milk. Repeat the process to obtain the second thin batch of coconut milk. After this the pulp can be discarded as there is absolutely nothing left in it.

If fresh coconut is not available, you can substitute coconut cream for the milk. Coconut cream is available in a solid pack at most good stores. Break off a small amount, add some hot water and, stirring it, dissolve the cream to the required consistency.

❧❦❧

Tamarind Water
Imli ka Pani

Although the two have nothing in common, tamarind has often been known as Indian date. Although the green tamarind pods are delicious in a chutney, it is usually the mature sticky brown pods that are used. Tamarind is usually sold in most Indian shops, either closely packed into 225g/8 oz packs or in a bottle as tamarind pulp concentrate. To prepare tamarind juice or water you need:-

Small piece of tamarind
Warm water

1. Pour the warm water over the tamarind and allow to soak for about 15 minutes.
2. Squeeze and rub the tamarind pulp between your fingers

in order to loosen all the brown sticky pulp adhering to the seeds and fibres.
3. Strain through a sieve. Discard any fibres and shells and the stone. Reserve the pulpy liquid.
4. Dilute according to the recipe.

Starters, Soups and Salads

Dishes such as kebabs, chicken, tikka or some tandoori varieties of foods from the traditional repertoire are often served with drinks or as appetizers in the modern way of thinking. I have purposely not made any mention of these in my book as I feel there are so many other, more original dishes that I would like you to sample and cook.

As the whole structure of an Indian meal has been broken up into different courses it is important to remember that all portions, no matter for which course, should be fairly small. First courses or starters should be just the right size to create an appetite and excitement for what is to follow. If large starters or first courses are served then the rest of the meal becomes an endurance test.

The dishes in this chapter are unique in the sense that the ingredients used are complementary to each other and also combine to create new tastes. Small prawns or shrimps lightly spiced and heated through with grapefruit segments, lamb spare ribs baked in tamarind sauce, or stir-fried chicken pieces with almonds are just a few samples of what the chapter contains. Great emphasis has been placed on the presentation of the dishes, whether served in individual portions or in a common dish: the final product should appear delicate so that the eater is not filled with a sense of foreboding and an overwhelming desire to leave half of it.

The spicing has been carefully selected so that the true flavours of the other ingredients are not smothered but enhanced.

It is in this chapter that I have included a handful of pulse soups which are lightly spiced to enhance the delicate yet bland taste of the pulse stock.

Salads are usually included as part of the main meal in the traditional way of serving Indian meals, but I have chosen to serve them as starters as they are too delicate to be included with anything else. The smoked salad (page 73) provides a unique experience, and the same principle can be applied to a whole range of spices, e.g. chillies, cloves etc.

<hr />

Fan-shaped Stuffed Fish Fillets
Bharve Machchi ke Panke

Fillets of sole, plaice or pomfret would be best suited for this delicate starter. The dark tomato-mushroom filling inside the white fillet served on a bed of finely shredded lettuce is a delight to the eye and the taste buds.

Serves 4
Preparation time: 30 minutes

52

Cooking time: 25 minutes

1 medium onion
1 clove of garlic
75g/3 oz button mushrooms
2 ripe tomatoes
2 tablespoons oil
1/2 teaspoon cumin seeds
1/2 teaspoon salt

1/4 teaspoon chilli powder
4 whole fillets of sole,
   skinned
4 crisp lettuce leaves
1 tablespoon finely chopped
   coriander leaves

Ask the fishmonger to skin and fillet the fish for you if you find it difficult. Although fresh fish would be better, frozen fillets can also be used. Use 2 fillet halves per person.

1. Finely chop the onion, crush the garlic, slice the mushrooms, skin, deseed and finely chop the tomatoes.
2. Heat the oil, add the cumin seeds, and as soon as they pop add the onion and garlic. Stir-fry to a pale golden colour.
3. Add the mushrooms, sauté for another minute, then add the tomatoes, salt and chilli powder.
4. Fry the mixture, stirring frequently, until the tomatoes are reduced to a pulp. Remove from the heat and tilt the pan slightly to pour off any excess oil.
5. Lightly grease an ovenproof dish, place one fillet in the dish, spread about 1 tablespoon of the mushroom and onion mixture on it, then fold the fillet lengthwise into half. Repeat with the remaining fillets and mixture.
6. Brush the fillets with a little oil, and bake in a preheated oven – gas 4/180°C/350°F – for about 25 minutes.
7. Cut the lettuce into fine shreds and spread on individual serving dishes.
8. Carefully lift the fish from the baking dish and transfer to the serving dishes.
9. Place a small pinch of fresh coriander leaves on top of each and serve at once.

Serving suggestion
Two stuffed fillet halves are just about enough per person. If you like lemon with fish, then serve a twist of lemon with the fish.

Freezing hint
Fully prepared fillets can be frozen successfully. Line each one with freezer paper to prevent them sticking together. There is no need to thaw before reheating: just remove the freezer paper, cover the dish with a lid and heat in the preheated oven for about 25 minutes or in a microwave for 3–4 minutes.

❧

Sweet and Sour Prawns in Grapefruit
Khate Meethe Jhinge

The large grapefruits are best for this dish. Although they are slightly different from those found in India, and slightly bitter, they are a good substitute. Use fresh or frozen prawns, which are cooked in an onion and garlic mixture, then piled back into the grapefruit shell, grilled and served.

Serves 4
Preparation time: 25 minutes
Cooking time: 25 minutes

2 large ripe grapefruit	1 tablespoon oil
1 medium onion	$^1/_2$ teaspoon salt
1 clove of garlic	$^1/_4$ teaspoon chilli powder
225g/8 oz fresh or frozen prawns (medium sized)	$^1/_2$ teaspoon sugar
1 ripe tomato	1 tablespoon finely chopped fresh coriander leaves

1 Cut the grapefruit in half. Using a grapefruit knife, carefully cut out the segments. Make sure you don't cut

into the skin. Discard the white pith around the segments and the pips. Place the segments in a bowl.

2. Finely chop the onion and crush the garlic. If fresh prawns are used, shell and devein them. If frozen, thaw out completely and pat dry on kitchen paper. Skin the tomato, remove its seeds and cut it into very small pieces.
3. Heat the oil, add the onion and garlic. Sauté until the onion turns transparent and soft but does not colour. Add the prawns, tomato, salt and chilli powder.
4. Stirring frequently, cook this mixture over high heat until the prawns are heated through and the tomato becomes soft.
5. Add the grapefruit segments, sugar and coriander leaves. Reduce the heat to medium setting and, stirring frequently, cook for another few minutes until the grapefruit segments are warmed through.
6. Pile the mixture into the empty grapefruit shells and serve at once.

Serving suggestion
An appetizing starter to any meal, especially during the cold days of winter. It can also serve as a substantial main salad dish along with spicy almond potatoes (page 132). Crab or lobster can be substituted for prawns.

<hr>

Pork Spare Ribs in Pepper Rings
Spare Ribs aur Mirch ke Chakkar

Barbecued spare ribs or sweet and sour pork ribs have now become an integral part of our enjoyment of good eating. For this dish I have baked the spare ribs with a honey and lemon glaze with just a hint of mint and green chilli. Coated with lightly toasted sesame seeds, they become a deliciously crunchy starter.

Serves 4
Preparation time: 25 minutes
Cooking time: 55 minutes

2 cloves of garlic
2 green chillies
1 teaspoon dried mint or 2
   tablespoons fresh mint
12 meaty spare ribs (3 per
   person)
3 tablespoons clear honey

3 tablespoons lemon juice
1 teaspoon salt
75g/3 oz sesame seeds
2 green peppers
2 red peppers
2 tablespoons oil

1. Finely grind the garlic, green chillies and mint.
2. Wash and dry the spare ribs.
3. Place the honey, lemon juice, garlic, green chilli and mint mixture and salt into an ovenproof baking dish. Mix the ingredients well together.
4. Add the spare ribs and completely coat them with the honey and lemon mixture.
5. Basting frequently, bake the spare ribs for about 45 minutes at gas 4/180°C/350°F. The meat should be tender and crisp.
6. Remove the spare ribs from the honey lemon sauce and coat them with the sesame seeds.
7. Place the spare ribs in a clean baking dish and bake for another 10 minutes, turning once. This will lightly roast the sesame seeds.
8. While the spare ribs are cooking, prepare the red and green peppers. Carefully slice the peppers into 0.5cm/^{1}/$_4$-inch thick rings. Remove and discard any white pith and seeds.
9. Heat the oil in a shallow frying pan. Add the pepper rings and gently sauté for a few minutes, making sure that they remain crisp. Drain and keep aside.
10. Once the sesame seeds have browned, remove from the oven and thread the spare ribs through the rings of peppers and serve at once.

Serve piping hot. To make the presentation attractive alternate the rings of green and red peppers. Serve any leftover sauce separately if required, although I feel the spare ribs taste better dry.

~~~=O=C=~~~

Layered Mince and Parantha
Lipta hua Keema aur Parantha

Although Italian in concept, the ingredients are very much Indian. Instead of using lasagne, I have used thin crisp paranthas which are layered with spicy mince and then baked. The paranthas should be small, no bigger than about 12.5cm/5 inches in diameter and no thicker than 0.5cm/¼ inch.

Serves 4
Preparation time: 20 minutes
Cooking time: 40 minutes

350g/12 oz fine mince
1 tablespoon oil
1 teaspoon cumin seeds
1 medium onion, finely chopped
1cm/½ inch fresh ginger, peeled and finely chopped
1 clove of garlic, finely chopped
1 green chilli, finely chopped
1 teaspoon salt
½ teaspoon chilli powder

¼ teaspoon turmeric
2 medium tomatoes, finely chopped
2 tablespoons lemon juice
150ml/¼ pint water
8 small crisp paranthas (page 213)
2 tablespoons Cheddar cheese, grated
½ teaspoon garam masala
1 tablespoon freshly chopped coriander leaves

Prepare the mince first, and while it is cooking make the paranthas.

1. Place the mince in a pan and break it up into fine pieces with a fork, for as it cooks it will stick into small lumps. Cover and cook until the mince turns brown. (Stir once or twice.)
2. Carefully strain it, then return the fat to the pan. Keep the mince warm.
3. Add the oil to the fat in the pan and heat it up. Sprinkle cumin seeds on to it, and as soon as they pop add the finely chopped onion, ginger, garlic and green chilli.
4. Stir-fry to a golden brown, then add salt, chilli powder and turmeric. Fry for another few seconds then add the tomatoes and lemon juice.
5. Stirring frequently, cook the mixture until the tomatoes are reduced to a pulp. Add the fried mince, stir well and pour in the water. Mix well, cover and cook over a low heat until the mince is tender and all the moisture has dried up.
6. Lightly grease a baking sheet and place a crisp parantha on it. Spread the mince over the parantha, place another on top, spread some more mince on top, then sprinkle some grated cheese over it. Repeat this process until all the paranthas, mince and cheese are used up. Sprinkle a pinch of garam masala on top of each portion.
7. Place in a hot oven – gas 6/200°C/400°F – for 10 minutes to melt the cheese.
8. Remove from the oven, sprinkle some coriander on top and serve.

Serving suggestion
Although in India mince is often eaten with paranthas, it is not usually piled up in this manner and then baked. So this recipe makes an interesting and different starter. It is very filling so can also be used for a substantial snack.

Freezing hint
Can be frozen successfully in its finished state. Thaw out completely before reheating.

Chicken Delight
Murghi Mazedar

For this delicious dish I have used slices of processed cheese, which is readily available in the West and now equally popular in India. Unlike the usual kebabs, which are first marinated and then simply grilled or barbecued, I have coated the chicken pieces in spicy coconut chutney, then wrapped a thin slice of cheese around each and skewered and grilled it over a barbecue. They can also be grilled, but care must be taken not to brown the cheese – just melt it slightly.

Serves 4
Preparation time: 30 minutes
Cooking time: 15 minutes

2 chicken breasts, skinned
2 green chillies
1 clove of garlic
100g/4 oz freshly grated
  coconut
¾ teaspoon salt
2 tablespoons natural yogurt
8 slices processed cheese
lettuce
cucumber

1. Cut each chicken breast into 4 equal rectangular portions.
2. Grind the green chillies and garlic, and mix them with the grated coconut, salt and the yogurt to a smooth consistency. (If desiccated coconut is used, soften it with a little warm water first, then add the other ingredients.)
3. This chutney should be really spicy – so taste it, as the green chillies can be quite mild at times (in which case increase the quantity of chillies).
4. Dip the chicken pieces into the chutney and completely coat them with it.
5. Carefully wrap a cheese slice around the chutney chicken (you may need to use 2 cheese slices per chicken portion).

Repeat until all the chutney and chicken have been used up.

6. If the chicken is to be grilled, place the cut edge on the underneath side on the tray (this will prevent it from opening up during cooking). Place the tray under a hot grill and cook for 10 minutes turning once so that the cheese begins to melt but does not brown.
7. If the chicken is to be barbecued, carefully pierce the skewer through the thickness and barbecue over a fierce heat so that the chicken cooks quickly without the cheese browning.
8. Cut the lettuce and cucumber into very fine shreds. Place cooked chicken on top and serve at once.

Serving suggestion
An excellent dish to be served with drinks, in which case the chicken can be cut up smaller and served on cocktail sticks.

◆━◦━◆

Saffron Roasted Chicken
Kesar Bhooni Murghi

Saffron, the most expensive spice on earth, is worth its weight in gold. The delicate aroma and colour that it emits is truly mouthwatering. Pieces of chicken breast marinated in saffron and other spices, then just tossed in oil, make an excellent starter to any meal.

Serves 4
Preparation time: 20 minutes plus 3 hours marinating
Cooking time: 15 minutes

3 chicken breasts
75ml/3 fl.oz warm milk
Large pinch of saffron
3 green cardamom pods
$^{1}/_{2}$ teaspoon freshly ground
   black pepper

1 teaspoon salt
4 tablespoons natural yogurt
2 tablespoons ghee or oil

1. Skin the chicken breasts and cut them into small bite-size pieces.
2. Warm the milk in a small pan and sprinkle saffron on top. Stir to infuse the saffron.
3. Remove the seeds from the cardamom pods and lightly crush them.
4. In a bowl, mix together all the ingredients except the ghee. Stir well to mix and completely coat the chicken pieces. Cover and leave to marinate for 3 hours. Remember to baste the chicken pieces three to four times.
5. Heat the ghee in a *karahi*. When really hot, add the marinated chicken pieces and the marinade and, stirring constantly, fry them over a high heat until they are tender and the yogurt has become a thickish sauce.
6. Serve at once.

Serving suggestion
Serve as a hot starter to the main meal.

⊷◦⊶

Hot Avocado and Chicken
Garam Murghi Malai me

I find avocado a delight to work with: because of its delicate but bland taste, it can combine with almost any other flavour. Although avocadoes are not commonly used in India except in the south where they grow as a fruit, I find that they combine very successfully with Indian spices, hence the creation of this dish.

Serves 4
Preparation time: 25 minutes
Cooking time: 30 minutes

1 small onion
1 clove of garlic
1 green chilli
1 chicken breast
2 large ripe avocadoes
$^3/_4$ teaspoon salt
25g/1 oz Cheddar cheese, coarsely grated
2 tablespoons corn oil
$^1/_2$ teaspoon cumin seeds

1. It is important that the onion is chopped very finely. Crush the garlic and very finely chop the green chilli. (If a medium hot dish is required then split the green chilli and remove the seeds.)
2. Remove the chicken skin and cut the breast into very small chunks, about 1cm/$^1/_2$ inch square.
3. Cut the avocadoes in half and remove the stones. Carefully scoop out the soft green flesh into a bowl, taking care not to damage the skin.
4. Mash the pulp with a fork until it is a fairly smooth consistency. Add the onion, garlic and green chilli, salt and Cheddar cheese. Mix the ingredients together.
5. Heat the oil in a shallow frying pan, add the cumin seeds, as soon as they splutter, add the chicken chunks. Stirring constantly, fry them to a pale golden colour.
6. Pour the avocado purée over the chicken and just bring it to the boil, then reduce the heat and continue cooking for another few minutes.
7. Remove from the heat, pile the hot chicken and avocado mixture back into the avocado shells and serve at once.

Serving suggestion
This dish is quite a substantial starter, so should be followed by a light main course.

Chicken with Almonds
Badami Murghi

Almonds add texture and crunchy flavour to any dish. In this instance the chicken breast is cut into bite-size pieces – just about the same size as the almonds – and stir-fried over high heat before any of the spices are added.

Serves 4
Preparation time: 15 minutes
Cooking time: 20 minutes

2 chicken breasts
2 cloves of garlic
Small piece of fresh ginger
2 tablespoons oil
50g/2 oz blanched whole almonds
1/2 teaspoon allspice

1/2 teaspoon freshly ground black pepper
1 1/4 teaspoons salt
1 tablespoon fresh lemon juice
1 tablespoon freshly chopped coriander leaves

1. Cut the chicken breasts into small bite-size pieces.
2. Crush the garlic, peel and finely chop the ginger.
3. Heat the oil in a frying pan or *kurahi*. Add the chicken and stir-fry over high heat until the chicken begins to brown.
4. Add all the listed ingredients except the lemon juice and coriander leaves.
5. Stir-fry over high heat until the chicken and almonds are well coated in the spices.
6. Add the lemon juice. Stir well for another few minutes. It is important to cook this uncovered, otherwise the chicken will release too much water.
7. Serve hot, sprinkled with the coriander leaves.

A delicious starter served with spicy mint chutney (page 252) or with a tossed green salad.

❖━◦━❖

Quick-fried Liver Marinated in Lemon Juice
Kaleji Nimboo Wali

When I was expecting my first baby I was advised to eat as much liver as possible. As I couldn't get to enjoy it, I developed this recipe which has since become a favourite not only with me but also my daughter.

Serves 4
Preparation time: 10 minutes
Cooking time: 5 minutes

275g/10 oz liver
Juice of 1 lemon
1 green chilli (optional)
Small piece of fresh ginger
1 clove of garlic

$3/4$ teaspoon salt
Freshly ground black pepper
1 tablespoon oil
1 tablespoon chopped fresh
   green coriander leaves

1. Cut the liver into 2.5cm/1-inch pieces. Place them in a bowl with the lemon juice.
2. Finely chop the green chilli and fresh ginger, and crush the garlic.
3. Add these to the liver and lemon juice along with the salt and pepper.
4. Stir well to coat the liver pieces in the juice. Leave in the refrigerator to marinate for 3–4 hours, or longer if possible.
5. Heat a frying pan. When hot, add the oil and after a few seconds add the liver and marinade. Increase the heat and, stirring continuously, fry the pieces until the lemon juice

has evaporated and the liver pieces are nicely glazed (this should not take more than 5 minutes).

6. Serve at once, sprinkled with the coriander leaves.

Serving suggestion
Serve with a nice mixed tossed salad. It can also be served on cocktail sticks as an interesting accompaniment with drinks.

Variation
The same delicious result can be achieved by substituting prawns or shrimps for liver.

❧

Kidneys Wrapped in Bacon
Bacon me Lipte hue Gurde

As a child I often used to visit a favourite uncle whose cook made the most delicious kidneys. They were not only tender and succulent, but had the most intriguing flavour. In those days I could never identify the flavour, but later on, as I became aware of ingredients not generally found in India, I realized that the unusual flavour came from bacon. The kidneys are first marinated in lemon juice and spices then wrapped in bacon and barbecued or grilled.

Serves 4–6
Preparation time: 15 minutes plus 1 hour marinating
Cooking time: 15 minutes

1 clove of garlic
1 green chilli
4 tablespoons lemon juice
1/4 teaspoon freshly milled
  black pepper

1 teaspoon salt
12 small lamb kidneys
12 rashers streaky bacon

1. Grind together the garlic and green chilli to make a fine paste.
2. Mix together the lemon juice, garlic and chilli paste, black pepper and salt.
3. Remove any membrane from the kidneys. Carefully make a deep incision into the kidney from the centre where the veins are connected, taking care not to cut through to the other side.
4. Place the kidneys in a bowl, pour the lemon juice mixture on top and leave to marinate for about 1 hour.
5. Remove from the marinade and very carefully wrap a bacon rasher around each kidney, then skewer it so that the bacon and kidney are held together. Place two kidneys on one skewer, not too close together.
6. Barbecue or grill them for about 8 minutes on each side.
7. Remove from the skewers and serve.

Serving suggestion
Serve piping hot either with drinks or as a starter. I like to serve these on a bed of very finely sliced onion rings dusted with salt and black pepper.

Black-eyed Beans with Mushrooms
Lobia aur Khumba

The delicious musky flavour of this pale cream-coloured bean is further enhanced by the use of fresh basil, a herb that is rarely used in Indian cooking, but grown in just about every household as a sacred plant. The only time it is used as a culinary herb is when it is brewed with other spices in tea, but only for its medicinal properties in curing colds and 'flu. The black-eyed bean is easy to cook as it is softer than beans in the rest of its family.

Serves 4–6
Preparation time: 20 minutes plus 3 hours soaking
Cooking time: 1^1/$_2$ hours (or quicker in a pressure cooker)

175g/6 oz black-eyed beans
750ml/1^1/$_4$ pints water
1^1/$_4$ teaspoons salt
2 medium onions
2.5cm/1-inch piece of fresh
  ginger, peeled
1 clove of garlic
2 green chillies

12–14 fresh basil leaves or 1
  teaspoon dried basil
100g/4 oz tomatoes
100g/4 oz button
  mushrooms
2 tablespoons oil
1 teaspoon mustard seeds
Small pinch of asafoetida

1. Clean and wash the black-eyed beans then soak them in
   plenty of cold water for about 3 hours.
2. Drain, wash again and place in a saucepan along with the
   water and half the salt. Bring to the boil then reduce the
   heat, cover and leave to cook for about an hour or until
   the beans are tender but retain their shape. (If a pressure
   cooker is used, follow the manufacturer's instructions or
   use the same amount of water and cook on high pressure
   for about 20 minutes.)
3. Drain off the water.
4. Finely slice the onions, ginger, garlic and green chillies.
   Wash, shake dry and chop the basil leaves. Wash and chop
   the tomatoes. Wash and wipe dry the mushrooms.
5. Heat the oil, add the mustard seeds and, as soon as they
   pop, add the asafoetida. This will fry at once, so
   immediately add the sliced onions, ginger, garlic and
   green chillies. Stirring continuously, fry this over high
   heat so that the onion becomes dark golden in colour.
6. Add the drained black-eyed beans, mushrooms, remaining salt, tomatoes and basil leaves.
7. Again over fairly high heat, stir and toss this mixture until
   the beans and mushrooms are blended with the other
   ingredients. Cook for about 10–15 minutes. As this dish
   should be dry, it is important that all the moisture be
   allowed to evaporate.

Serving suggestion
This quantity of beans is enough to serve 4–6 people either for a separate course with crisp pooris (page 224) or as part of the main course with a crisp pork *raita* (page 199) and rice.

Freezing hint
Excellent for freezing. Freeze in small portions. When needed, completely thaw, then heat a tablespoon of oil in a frying pan, add the thawed black-eyed beans and stir-fry over high heat for about 5 minutes. Serve hot at once.

Onion and Lime Salad
Piaz ka Salat

A favourite of mine which goes well with a lot of dishes. A simple salad to make, it should be prepared only a few minutes in advance.

Serves 4
Preparation time: 5 minutes

 2 medium onions   ½ teaspoon salt
½ lemon or lime
Dash of freshly milled black
  pepper

  1. Peel the onions and thinly slice them into rings.
  2. Separate the layers. Add salt and pepper, squeeze lemon or lime juice on top and mix well.
  3. Serve at once because the onion starts to smell after a while.

Sweet Potato and Almond Salad
Shakarkandi Badam Wali

Although the Americans are quite used to sweet potatoes, in the UK they are still a novelty, and until recently could only be bought in oriental grocery stores. A root vegetable belonging to the potato family, it has a deep pink skin (not unlike the red potatoes) and a slightly off-white fibrous flesh with a mild nutty and sweetish flavour. A vegetable worth trying; buy small ones if possible.

Serves 4–6
Preparation time: 30 minutes
Cooking time: 40 minutes

450g/1 lb sweet potatoes
100g/4 oz streaky bacon
2 tablespoons oil
50g/2 oz blanched almonds
1 teaspoon cumin seeds

1 teaspoon ground coriander
1/2 teaspoon chilli powder
1 teaspoon salt
1 teaspoon dried mint

1. Thoroughly wash the sweet potatoes and boil until tender. (It is important not to let the skins split.)
2. When cool, peel then cut into small chunks.
3. Remove the bacon's rind and cut into small pieces.
4. Heat the oil, add the blanched almonds and bacon and fry to a crisp golden colour.
5. Add the cumin seeds and as soon as they pop add the rest of the spices, salt and mint. Stir-fry for a second then add the sweet potato chunks and fry, stirring continuously, until the chunks are coated with the spices.
6. Serve hot.

Serve hot as a starter or as a hot salad. A delicious and substantial dish.

❧

Chickpea Salat
Kabli Channe ka Salad

A very refreshing and filling salad which can be served either hot or cold.

Serves 4
Preparation time: 10 minutes
Cooking time: 40 minutes

175g/6 oz chickpeas
1/4 teaspoon bicarbonate of soda
Small piece of fresh ginger
1 medium onion
1 small green chilli (optional)
Small bunch of fresh green coriander leaves

1/2 small cucumber or 1 green pepper
1/2 teaspoon garam masala
1 teaspoon salt
1 1/2 tablespoons oil
1 teaspoon cumin seeds

Dressing
2 tablespoons olive oil or salad oil
4–5 tablespoons wine vinegar
Dash of Worcestershire sauce

1 teaspoon sugar
1/2 teaspoon salt
1/2 teaspoon chilli powder
Pinch of mustard powder
1/2 teaspoon dried mint
Pinch of garlic powder

1. Leave the chickpeas to soak overnight in plenty of cold water. They should swell up to twice their size.
2. Drain and discard any discoloured peas. Place them in a

pressure cooker, add the bicarbonate of soda. Stir well. Cover and cook under pressure for about 15–20 minutes. The chickpeas should be tender but whole. Drain and keep aside.

3. Peel and finely chop the ginger, onion, green chilli and coriander leaves. Keep aside. Cube the cucumber or deseed the pepper and cut into small cubes.

4. Place the drained chickpeas in a large salad bowl. Add the ginger, onions, green chilli, coriander leaves and the cucumber or green pepper along with the garam masala and salt. Thoroughly mix everything together.

5. Heat the oil in a frying pan, then add the cumin seeds. As soon as they pop pour this over the chickpea mixture.

6. The dressing can be prepared in advance, and should be added to the salad about 10–15 minutes before serving.

7. In a clean jar add all the ingredients required for the dressing. Screw on the lid and shake vigorously, so that the oil, vinegar and spices infuse properly. If the dressing has been made well in advance, then shake the bottle again before adding it to the chickpea salad.

Serving suggestion
I find that this salad is equally delicious whether served hot or cold.

Freezing hint
Boiled, drained chickpeas can be frozen very satisfactorily. After thawing out completely, reheat them thoroughly, then add all the other ingredients. Again, serve hot or cold.

Crisp Cabbage, Carrot and Green Pepper Salad
Kachu Paku

A salad with a difference. Recently, while travelling in the western region of India, I came across some very light and refreshing dishes which have been around for quite some time but seem to have got lost in the traditional cooking. Here is a salad that has a hot garnish added just before serving.

Serves 4
Preparation time: 15 minutes

100g/4 oz fresh crisp green cabbage
2 medium-sized carrots
2 green peppers
1 teaspoon salt
Freshly ground black pepper

2 tablespoons lemon juice
1 tablespoon oil
1 teaspoon mustard seeds
Small pinch of asafoetida
Small pinch of sugar
1 green chilli, finely chopped

1. Thoroughly wash and shake dry the cabbage. Shred it finely. Scrape and cut carrots into thin julienne strips. Remove the stalks, seeds and pith from the peppers and cut into thin strips.
2. Place the prepared vegetables into a salad bowl and add the salt, freshly ground black pepper and lemon juice.
3. Heat the oil then add the mustard seeds. As soon as they pop and splutter, add the asafoetida, sugar and chilli.
4. Stir-fry for a few seconds, pour the garnish over the prepared salad, toss well and serve at once.

Note: It is important that the hot garnish be poured on at the last minute, otherwise the salad will become limp and unappetizing.

An excellent starter to a meal, or as a side salad with a main course.

❧

Smoked Salad
Dhuan ka Salat

The inspiration for this salad came to me one night during a recent visit to the beautiful, lush area of Goa. Talking about new salads to the chefs at the hotel, a vision of spicy smoked salad came to mind. Although no visible spice is added to the salad, it still has the definite taste of it. Let me unfold the mystery. Any spice of your taste is placed on the naked flame; as it starts smoking, the aroma and smoke are captured in an inverted jar held over it, and the salad is tossed in it.

Serves 4
Preparation time: 20–25 minutes
Cooking time: 5 minutes

$^1/_2$ crisp iceberg lettuce
2 crisp celery stalks
1 large green pepper
1 medium red pepper
$^1/_2$ teaspoon salt
$^1/_2$ teaspoon freshly milled
   black pepper

1 tablespoon fresh lemon
   juice
5cm/2-inch stick of
   cinnamon

1. Thoroughly wash and shake dry the lettuce leaves. Cut into thick strips about 1cm/$^1/_2$ inch thick.
2. Wash the celery and cut into 0.5cm/$^1/_4$ inch slices.
3. Remove the stalks, seeds and pith from the peppers, keeping them whole. Then cut into thin rounds.

4. Place the vegetables in a bowl and add the salt, black pepper and lemon juice. Toss well.
5. Place the cinnamon stick over a naked flame and allow it to start smoking. As soon as the smoke starts, hold a large screw-top glass jar upside down over the smoke, so that it is trapped in the jar.
6. Quickly transfer the prepared salad into the smoke-filled glass jar, close the lid and shake for a minute or two.
7. Serve the salad at once, otherwise it will go limp.

Serving suggestion
A very delicate salad which needs no other accompaniment, except perhaps a thoroughly chilled dry white wine.

━━◗○◖━━

Almond Soup
Badam ka Shorba

Sitting in the roof-top restaurant at the beautiful Maurya Hotel in New Delhi, one has time to contemplate the good things in life. On one occasion, as usual the topic of conversation among my guests (who happened to be the hotel chefs) and myself was food. The master chef promised me a dish which I would not forget in a hurry. The result when it was presented to me was the most delicate almond soup, the taste of which still hovers in my mouth.

Serves 4
Preparation time: 40 minutes plus 30 minutes soaking
Cooking time: 15 minutes

175g/6 oz shelled almonds
150ml/^{1}/$_4$ pint milk
750ml/1^1/$_4$ pints rich chicken stock

^{1}/$_2$ teaspoon salt
Dash of white pepper
1 tablespoon almond slivers

1. Soak the almonds in warm water for half an hour so that they absorb some of the moisture. Peel off the skins and place the almonds in a liquidizer along with the milk. Add some chicken stock if the almond paste is too thick for the blades to move freely.
2. Heat the chicken stock, without boiling, then add the almond and milk paste. Give the mixture a good stir.
3. Season with the salt and white pepper.
4. Lightly roast the almond slivers for about 2–3 minutes, turning them over once.
5. Pour the soup into warmed individual serving bowls, sprinkle a few of the roasted almond slivers on top and serve.

Note: Don't serve the soup piping hot as that will ruin the delicate aroma and flavour of the almonds.

✂══●══✃

Moath Bean Soup
Moath ka Shorba

The liquid that has been strained from boiled moath beans can be used for a thin soup, but if a thicker soup is required then liquidize the beans to a smooth consistency.

Serves 4–6
Preparation time: 10 minutes
Cooking time: 1 hour

100g/4 oz moath beans   1 clove of garlic
1 litre/1³/₄ pints water   1 green chilli
1 teaspoon salt

Garnish (Tarka)

2 tablespoons ghee
1 teaspoon cumin seeds
2 tablespoons natural
    yogurt, lightly whipped

1 tablespoon finely chopped
    coriander leaves

1. Thoroughly wash the moath beans in a few changes of water.
2. Place in a saucepan along with the water, salt, garlic and green chilli.
3. Cover and bring to the boil, then keep boiling gently until tender. (If using a pressure cooker, follow the manufacturer's instructions.)
4. Cool slightly, transfer to a food processor or liquidizer and purée to a smooth consistency.
5. Transfer back to the saucepan, reheat and adjust the salt level.
6. Pour into a soup tureen or individual soup bowls and prepare the *tarka*.
7. Heat the ghee in a shallow pan. Add the cumin seeds, and as soon as they pop remove from the heat and allow to cool for a minute or two.
8. Add the yogurt and mix well.
9. Carefully pour the *tarka* over the soup, making an attractive design.
10. Sprinkle finely chopped coriander leaves on top and serve at once.

⊂⊃•⊂⊃

Black Chickpea Soup
Kale Channe ka Shorba

The shrivelled-up black chickpea doesn't look very appetizing, but after it has been soaked overnight and boiled, it is transformed beyond the humble pea of its origin. Black chickpea is one of the richest protein-containing pulses, hence its soup is often given to invalids to build up their strength.

Serves 4
Preparation time: 10 minutes plus 24 hours soaking
Cooking time: 1½ hours

225g/8 oz black chickpea
1 litre/1¾ pints water
1cm/½ inch fresh ginger,
  peeled

1 clove of garlic
1 teaspoon salt
Freshly ground black pepper

Garnish (Tarka)
1 tablespoon ghee
½ teaspoon cumin seeds
1 medium onion, finely
  sliced
1cm/½ inch fresh ginger,
  peeled and finely shredded

1 green chilli, finely chopped
1 tablespoon finely chopped
  fresh coriander leaves

1. Thoroughly clean the black chickpeas and wash in a couple of changes of water. Leave to soak in plenty of fresh water for at least 24 hours.
2. Drain off the water, rinse the chickpeas once more, then place them in a large saucepan with the water, peeled ginger and garlic (or pressure-cook them, following the manufacturer's instructions).
3. Bring the chickpeas to the boil, then reduce the heat slightly and simmer until they are completely tender but still retain their shape. (Add more water if necessary.)
4. Strain the liquid into another saucepan and add the salt and black pepper.
5. Pour the soup into individual dishes or a soup tureen.
6. To prepare the *tarka*, first heat the ghee then add the cumin seeds. As soon as they pop, add the onion and ginger.

77

7. Stir-fry to a rich golden brown, add the green chilli and at once pour the *tarka* over the soup.
8. Serve piping hot, garnished with coriander.

Serving suggestion
A rich soup to be served on a cold day.

Meat and Poultry

India is a country where most of the world's religions exist side by side, consequently there are various taboos attached to the eating of meat. The Hindus don't eat beef, the Muslims don't eat pork, the Buddhists won't slaughter animals themselves, and so on. But despite the taboos, meat cookery has been developed to a very sophisticated art, with distinct regional varieties. And common to all Indians is a dislike of the raw taste of meat. Unlike Westerners who enjoy steak that is rare or medium done, the Indians prefer meat to be *'bhoona'* – well fried or roasted, really tender without much bite left in it. For this reason meats are traditionally marinated in a mixture of spices and cooked over a low heat for hours, in enough fat to prevent burning or sticking to the pan. Consequently the dish is fairly rich and the fat content high. It is with these facts in mind that I have created the recipes for this chapter.

I feel most meats contain enough natural fat for there to be no need to add more. Hence the dishes in this chapter are cooked in their own fat and juices. Traditional meat dishes such as Rogan Josh or kormas of various kinds contain as many as ten to fifteen spices. Although the result is delicious, it is very difficult to separate the taste of spices that have blended together so beautifully. So I have used only two or three spices in each dish. Hence the recipes in this section are different from traditional meat dishes.

Fruit juices and purées are seldom used in traditional cooking, which is indeed a shame. I find that acidic fruit juices form an excellent marinade similar to lemon juice or even yogurt, so what could be better than thick lamb chops marinated in fresh orange juice and then baked slowly in the oven with just a hint of aniseed as the main spice. Fruit is also excellent as a sauce for meat, as in the recipe for sautéed pork chops served with mango purée. Ovens are not commonly available in India apart from the *tandoor*, which is too specialized for everyone to use, therefore most dishes are cooked over the hob. I have created dishes with the equipment available in the West (and slowly being made available in India). Oven cookery imparts a different taste to the dish. Imagine a leg of lamb which is stuffed with a spicy mint chutney, glazed with honey and roasted slowly for a few hours.

I have used stuffings such as spicy stoned dates, or apricot rice with aniseed, for duck and chicken with very little other flavouring, thus giving the whole dish a fresh taste and unique flavour. Sweet and sour tastes such as a mixture of honey and lemon with some ajowan seeds forms a different marinade for chicken that is baked in an oven or can be removed from the marinade and barbecued.

The reason for the marinade is twofold: it allows the spices to penetrate deeply; and it tenderizes the meat or poultry. Chicken has become popular in India only recently; until then, lamb and mutton were the most popular meats. The lamb or

80

mutton recipes in this chapter can easily be used for beef if that is preferred. The dishes here adopt a fresh approach to the whole idea of spicing meat and poultry so that the uniqueness of that particular spice is brought out to the full advantage. Very few dishes in the chapter are based on the traditional concept of the thick and rich onion, ground ginger and garlic base. The meat or poultry is gently sautéed first, then other ingredients such as fresh green and red peppers, or slivers of ginger are added, and stir-fried the Chinese way not only to cook quickly but also to retain the vegetables' crispness.

❖❖❖

Leg of Lamb Stuffed with Spicy Mint Chutney
Kubba Podina Raan

Spicy mint chutney is stuffed inside the leg of lamb, glazed with honey and baked in a slow oven until the meat literally falls off the bone.

Serves 4
Preparation time : 30 minutes
Cooking time: 1¹/₂ hours

1 1¹/₂kg/3 lb leg of lamb or
   mutton
100g/4 oz clear honey

50g/2 oz melted ghee
Juice of 2 lemons

Mint chutney
2 medium onions
2 large bunches of fresh mint
100g/4 oz dried pomegranate
   seeds

2 green chillies
1¹/₂ teaspoons salt

1. Remove all the fat from the leg of lamb or mutton. Wash and dry the meat thoroughly.
2. Using a sharp knife, make deep incisions going right down to the bone. Set aside on a deep baking or roasting dish.
3. Peel and roughly chop the onions. Remove tough stalks from the mint, wash and shake dry. Remove the stalk end of the green chillies.
4. Place pomegranate seeds in a strainer and thoroughly but gently wash the seeds. Remove any fibres and tough pomegranate shells.
5. Place the onions, mint leaves, green chillies, pomegranate seeds and salt in a processor and liquidize to a smooth purée. Add a little water if necessary to get a smooth consistency. (The seeds will remain in tiny fragments as they are too hard to crush completely.)
6. Stuff this spicy chutney into the incisions in the lamb or mutton. Use up all the chutney.
7. Mix together the honey, melted ghee and lemon juice in a small bowl.
8. Brush this mixture liberally over both sides of the lamb.
9. Place the lamb in a preheated oven – gas 3/170°C/325°F – and cook for 1¹/₂ hours, turning once.
10. Frequently baste the leg with the honey and lemon mixture so as to achieve a perfect glaze.
11. Transfer the leg to a serving platter. Carve some up into thick slices and serve the rest uncarved, ready for carving when required.

Serving suggestion
Serve as part of the main course with a simple ginger rice (page 190), natural yogurt (page 47) and a mixed vegetable dish (page 143).

Freezing hint
Can be frozen very successfully either whole or cut into slices. Thaw out completely before reheating.

Stir-fried Lamb
with Fresh Fenugreek Leaves
Methi Wala Gosht

This stir-fried dish uses tender pieces of lamb which are first marinated in lemon juice and spices, then stir-fried over high heat for a few minutes. When the meat is nearly done, add the marinade and freshly chopped fresh fenugreek leaves.

Serves 4
Preparation time: 20 minutes plus 4–5 hours marinating
Cooking time: 30 minutes

450g/1 lb tender lamb (cut from the leg)
Juice of 2 lemons
5cm/2-inch piece of fresh ginger
1 clove of garlic
100g/4 oz fresh fenugreek leaves

1 green chilli (optional)
2 tablespoons oil
1 teaspoon ajowan seeds
$1/2$ teaspoon chilli powder
1 teaspoon salt

1. Trim off any excess fat from the meat and wipe it dry. Cut it into 2.5cm/1-inch cubes. It is very important that the meat is cut against the grain, otherwise on cooking the meat will be tough and fibrous.
2. Place the meat pieces in a bowl along with the lemon juice.
3. Peel and finely shred half the ginger and crush the garlic, and add both to the meat and lemon juice. Give it a good stir, cover and leave to marinate in the refrigerator for 4–5 hours – the longer the better, as the lemon juice helps to tenderize the meat.

83

4. Start cooking this dish about 15 minutes before you want to eat, as it has to be served at once.
5. Finely shred the rest of the ginger then strain the meat from the marinade, reserving the lemon juice.
6. Thoroughly wash and shake dry the fenugreek leaves. Chop them coarsely. Finely chop the green chilli if using.
7. Heat a frying pan or *karahi* to a high temperature. Hold the palm of your hand about 3 inches above the top. If it feels hot then the pan is ready to use.
8. Add the oil and heat for a few seconds. Take care not to let the oil smoke as it will ruin the flavour of the meat.
9. Add the ajowan seeds and as soon as they pop add the ginger.
10. Stir-fry for a minute, taking care not to let the ginger brown. Add the strained meat pieces and stir-fry quickly over high heat for 10 minutes. Add the chilli powder and the salt. Continue stir-frying until the pieces are well browned. Add the lemon juice and the fenugreek leaves and green chilli. Keep on stir-frying for another few minutes until the lemon juice has evaporated and the fenugreek leaves have cooked. (If the meat feels tough add a little water, cover and cook for a few minutes until tender.) Serve at once in a heated dish to retain its full flavour.

Sweet Tamarind and Mint Chops
Meethi Imli aur Podina Chops

New Delhi has an abundance of large shady trees which line the streets. One street in particular has large tamarind trees which in the summer bear the large firm green tamarind pods. It was these sour pods, eaten on the way home from school, that made me go hungry on many occasions as my teeth were too sour to chew or bite into anything else. The dark pulpy slab that is commercially produced is partly dried pods with the pips removed.

Serves 4
Preparation time: 35 minutes plus 2 hours marinating
Cooking time: 45–50 minutes

100g/4 oz tamarind pulp
8–10 lamb or mutton chops
1 medium onion, finely chopped or minced
2 cloves of garlic, crushed
2.5cm/1-inch piece of fresh ginger, finely chopped or minced
1 teaspoon garam masala

1 teaspoon chilli powder
50g/2 oz fresh, coarsely chopped coriander leaves
1½ teaspoons salt
2 tablespoons sugar
1 teaspoon roasted ground cumin seeds
450ml/¾ pint warm water

1. Place the tamarind pulp in a mixing bowl. Pour about 300ml/½ pint warm water into the pulp and leave to soak for about 15 minutes.
2. Remove excess fat from the chops and flatten them slightly.
3. Place them in an ovenproof dish.
4. With your fingers, loosen the tamarind pulp. Strain through a fairly open sieve. Discard the fibres and any tough bits. (Reserve the tamarind liquid.) Add the rest of the water to dilute the tamarind pulp.
5. Add all the ingredients to the tamarind liquid, check the seasoning in case a little more salt or sugar is needed according to individual taste.
6. Pour the liquid over the chops and completely immerse them. Leave to marinate for 2 hours, turning the chops once or twice.
7. Heat the oven to gas 3/170°C/325°F. Place the dish in it and, basting frequently, cook for 40–50 minutes or until the chops are tender and the marinade has thickened slightly.

Serve hot as a starter with onion rings sprinkled on top, or as a main dish with chappati (page 211) and onion rings.

Freezing hint
These chops freeze well. Thaw and reheat thoroughly before serving.

◀━▶◦◀━▶

Baked Lamb Chops in Orange Juice
Mausami ke Rus me Chops

An exciting combination of fresh orange juice, black pepper and lightly ground aniseed in which the thick lamb chops are first marinated and then baked in a slow oven. If the orange juice is too sharp then add some fine brown sugar, jaggery or clear honey to sweeten it. Just the right dish on a cold wintery night, in which case I add some rum or sherry towards the end of cooking. Thicken the sauce by boiling it to almost nothing.

Serves 4
Preparation time: 15 minutes plus 2 hours marinating
Cooking time: 1¹/₄ hours

8 thick meaty lamb chops
300ml/¹/₂ pint fresh orange juice
2 tablespoons aniseeds, lightly crushed
¹/₂ teaspoon chilli powder
¹/₂ teaspoon freshly ground black pepper
2 teaspoons brown sugar or clear honey (optional)

2.5cm/1-inch piece of fresh ginger, peeled and grated or ground
1 teaspoon salt
¹/₂ teaspoon garam masala
2 tablespoons sherry or rum (optional)

1. Trim any excess fat from the chops. Flatten them slightly with a meat hammer.
2. Pour the orange juice into a jug, add all the ingredients and stir well to mix so that the sugar or honey dissolves.
3. Place the lamb chops in a shallow ovenproof dish, pour the orange juice mixture on top and leave to marinate for 2 hours.
4. Place the dish in a preheated oven – gas 3/170°C/325°F – and, basting frequently, roast until the chops are really tender.
5. As a certain amount of fat will be released from the chops, carefully skim it off with a spoon.
6. Place the chops on a serving dish. Pour the sauce into a pan and boil rapidly to reduce it to half the quantity.
7. Pour the sauce over the chops and serve.

Serving suggestion
An excellent and unusual dish which is best served with rice and a crisp okra yogurt (page 204) and fresh green salad.

✦⊃◦⊂✦

Chops Baked in Onions and Spices
Dilruba Chops

A variation of the classic dish where the 'masala' spice and onion mixture is first fried to a rich brown and then the meat is added afterwards. In this recipe I have cut out the frying stage completely, baking the chops instead to produce an equally delicious result without the need for any additional fat.

Serves 4
Preparation time: 20 minutes plus 2 hours marinating
Cooking time: 1$^{1}/_{4}$ hours

225g/8 oz onions
2.5cm/1-inch piece of fresh
   ginger, peeled
2 cloves of garlic
2 tablespoons tomato purée
2 tablespoons natural yogurt
1 tablespoon lightly crushed
   aniseeds

1 teaspoon garam masala
1 teaspoon chilli powder
1¼ teaspoons salt
1kg/2 lbs lean mutton or
   lamb chops
1 tablespoon freshly
   chopped coriander leaves

1. Place all the listed ingredients except the chops and coriander in a food processor or blender and blend to smooth purée.
2. Trim off any excess fat from the chops. Wash and dry them with absorbent paper.
3. Place the chops in a shallow ovenproof dish. Cover completely with the onion mixture and leave to marinate for about 2 hours. Remember to turn the chops over once or twice.
4. Cover and bake in a preheated oven – gas 3/170°C/325°F – for about 1¼ hours.
5. Baste regularly with the juices from the meat, and remove the lid halfway through the cooking. Turn the chops over once.
6 Serve sprinkled with coriander.

Serving suggestion
Serve piping hot with nan (page 222) and okra in yogurt (page 204) and salad.

❧❀❧

Lamb Spare Ribs in Tamarind Sauce
Spare Ribs aur Imli ka Milan

Spare ribs are usually associated with Chinese cooking, but I find that if they are first marinated and then baked or shallow-fried, they make a delicious contribution to a meal. These spare ribs can quite easily be barbecued.

Serves 4
Preparation time: 20 minutes plus 4–5 hour marinating
Cooking time: 10–30 minutes, depending on the style of cooking

1kg/2 lbs spare ribs	$1/2$ teaspoon garam masala
50g/2 oz tamarind	1 teaspoon chilli powder
1 tablespoon sugar	$1^1/2$ teaspoons salt
1 tablespoon dried mint	A little oil for basting

1. Select small, meaty spare ribs and get the butcher to cut them into individual ribs. If that is not possible, buy portions with about 4–5 ribs joined together. One such portion per person should be enough.
2. Thoroughly remove any excess fat from the ribs, wash and dry them. Put on one side.
3. Soak the tamarind in about $1/2$ pint of warm water for about 10 minutes. Using your fingers, work the pulp loose to form the juice. Strain, reserve the juice and discard any stones and fibres.
4. Dilute this juice a little if too thick. Add all the other ingredients except the oil. Stir well.
5. Pour the tamarind juice and spice mixture on to the spare ribs, completely covering them. Cover and leave in the refrigerator to marinate for at least 4–5 hours. Longer if possible.
6. If the spare ribs are to be baked in the oven, glaze them with a little oil and place the dish in a warm oven – gas 3/170°C/325°F – for 30–40 minutes, remembering to baste frequently. Cook until the meat is tender and some of the sauce has evaporated. Serve hot with any remaining sauce poured over them.
7. If they are to be barbecued, strain the juice and reserve. Place the spare ribs on a prepared barbecue grill. Baste them frequently with oil and the reserved sauce.

8. If they are to be quick-fried, it is important that they are cut into individual ribs as it will make frying and stirring much easier. Strain the juice and reserve it. Heat a heavy-bottomed frying pan. When hot, add about 2–3 tablespoons of oil and then the strained spare ribs. Increase the heat and fry them, stirring continuously, for about 10 minutes until the spare ribs are crisp and brown.

Serving suggestion
The strained juice can be served as a dip along with the fried spare ribs.

Freezing hint
The cooked spare ribs freeze well. To reheat, thaw them out thoroughly then wrap in foil and heat in an oven.

◆►◄◆

Tasty Mango Mutton
Ambi aur Gosht ka Sawad

Dried mango powder is often used in vegetarian and in non-vegetarian dishes. In this recipe I have chosen to use fresh, half-ripe mango with other aromatic spices to enhance and complement the various aromas and flavours.

Serves 4
Preparation time: 25 minutes
Cooking time: 50 minutes

450g/1 lb mutton, lamb or beef
3 medium-sized half-ripe mangoes
2.5cm/1-inch piece of fresh ginger
2 cloves of garlic

3 small whole red chillies
4 green cardamom pods
4 tablespoons natural yogurt
2 tablespoons oil
$\frac{1}{2}$ teaspoon turmeric
$1\frac{1}{4}$ teaspoons salt

1. Remove any excess fat from the meat. Cut into small cubes. Wash and thoroughly dry the meat.
2. Peel and coarsely grate the mangoes. Discard the large stones.
3. Peel the ginger and grind it into a fine paste with the garlic, red chillies and 1 tablespoon of the grated mango.
4. Remove the cardamom seeds from their pods and coarsely grind the seeds.
5. Mix together the yogurt and the rest of the grated mango.
6. Heat the oil, add the ginger paste and stir-fry over medium heat for a minute.
7. Add the cardamom seeds, stir-fry for another few seconds then add the meat. Increase the heat slightly and, stirring continuously, fry the meat for about 10 minutes until it becomes golden brown.
8. Sprinkle the turmeric and salt over the meat, mix well and continue frying for another 5 minutes.
9. Pour in the mango and yogurt mixture. Stir well to blend all the ingredients.
10. Reduce the heat to low, cover with a tight-fitting lid and leave to cook for about 35–40 minutes until the meat is tender and the sauce has thickened slightly.

Serving suggestion
A delicious tangy dish best served with rice and a simple dal preparation.

Bitter Gourd Stuffed with Mince
Keema Karela

Bitter gourd is a vegetable that takes some getting used to. It is a boat-shaped green vegetable with a knobbly skin. Inside it is white with large edible seeds. The only drawback to this vegetable is that it is extremely bitter, hence its name, but that can easily be rectified by liberally coating it with salt and leaving it to drain for a few hours. Then wash thoroughly and use.

Serves 4
Preparation time: 20 minutes plus 4–5 hours draining
Cooking time: 1 hour

8 medium-sized tender bitter
  gourds
salt for coating
225g/8 oz minced meat
3 ripe tomatoes, chopped
1 teaspoon ground cumin

1 teaspoon ground coriander
1 teaspoon garam masala
1/2 teaspoon chilli powder
1 teaspoon salt
3 tablespoons oil

1. Scrape the knobbly green skin off the bitter gourds. Make a slit lengthwise along one side of the bitter gourds. Carefully remove all the white flesh and seeds inside, so that only a hollow skin remains.
2. Thoroughly coat the bitter gourds with plenty of salt inside and out. Place in a colander and allow to stand for 4–5 hours. This will extract any excess bitterness.
3. In the meantime prepare the mince by placing the mince, tomatoes, spices and salt in a saucepan and allow to cook in its own fat for 20–30 minutes. By this time the mince will have browned and become tender. Leave until cool enough to handle comfortably.
4. Wash the bitter gourds thoroughly under a running tap, to remove all traces of salt.

5. Carefully open the bitter gourds and stuff them with the mince mixture. Wind a length of cotton thread around the bitter gourds so that they do not open up during cooking.
6. Heat the oil in a frying pan. Add the stuffed bitter gourds and, turning occasionally, allow them to cook until golden in colour and tender.
7. Unwind and discard the cotton thread.

Serving suggestion
Serve as part of the main meal where no other meat or poultry dish has been included.

❦

Quick Mince Kebabs
Jaldi me Banaye hue Kabab

The traditional mince kebabs, although very delicious, do require a fair amount of preparation: the mince has first to be boiled with spices, then ground and finally recooked into kebabs. In this recipe I have eliminated all that preparation and made equally delicious kebabs in what I call the one-step method. All the ingredients are finely minced in a food processor or blender, then skewered and grilled or barbecued.

Serves 4
Preparation time: 15 minutes
Cooking time: 15 minutes

2.5cm/1-inch piece of fresh ginger
1 clove of garlic
2 green chillies
450g/1 lb lean mince

1 teaspoon dried mint
1 teaspoon garam masala
1 teaspoon salt
2 tablespoons oil

1. Peel the ginger and garlic and cut them into pieces. Remove the stalks from the chillies and cut the chillies into small pieces.
2. Place all the listed ingredients in a food processor or blender and mince to a fine paste.
3. Divide the mince into 8 portions and roll out into long sausage shapes, then chill for about 15 minutes.
4. Or mould the mince around 8 skewers and then chill for 15 minutes.
5. Brush with a very little oil, and grill over a barbecue or under a grill for 15 minutes, turning once.
6. Remove from the skewers and serve.

Serving suggestion
Serve with paranthas and yogurt with peppers (page 205) as a quick meal, or with a green tossed salad and yogurt mint chutney (page 252) as a starter.

◆⊃◦⊂◆

Pork Chops in Mango Purée
Aam ka Gosht

As pork is not readily available in India, due to the hot climate and also because of religious taboos, not many dishes have been tried with it. The quality of pork being excellent in the West, I have taken this opportunity to create a dish using thick pork chops which are cooked in a mouthwatering mango purée sauce.

Serves 4
Preparation time: 20 minutes
Cooking time: 30 minutes

4 pork chops, each 4cm/1$\frac{1}{2}$ inches thick
1 medium onion
225g/8 oz button mushrooms
2 tablespoons oil
2 tablespoons butter
1 tablespoon lightly crushed aniseeds
$\frac{1}{2}$ teaspoon freshly ground black pepper

1 tablespoon freshly chopped fennel or dill leaves
300ml/$\frac{1}{2}$ pint canned mango purée
150ml/$\frac{1}{4}$ pint water
1 teaspoon salt
2 tablespoons medium dry sherry

1. Trim off any excess fat from the pork chops. Flatten them slightly with a wooden meat hammer.
2. Finely chop the onion and finely slice the mushrooms into chefs' hats.
3. Heat the oil and butter in a frying pan until the butter starts to froth.
4. Add the pork chops and fry over gentle heat until they turn a rich golden colour. (Be careful not to overcook or the chops will become hard.)
5. Lift from the frying pan and keep warm.
6. Strain off all but 2 tablespoons of fat. Add the onion and sauté until soft and transparent, but not brown.
7. Select about 20 perfectly sliced mushrooms and keep aside. Add the rest to the sautéed onions and stir-fry to a pale golden colour.
8. Add the aniseed and freshly milled black pepper and stir-fry for another few seconds.
9. Mix together the mango purée, water and salt. Add this to the sautéed onions and mushrooms, and, stirring constantly, bring the sauce to simmering point. Add the sherry and stir it in.
10. Add the sautéed pork chops. Coat with the sauce, cover and leave to simmer gently for 10 minutes or until the chops have absorbed some of the sauce, and the sauce has reduced to half its quantity.

11. Heat the strained fat in a small frying pan. Gently sauté the 20 mushroom slices to a rich golden colour.
12. Transfer the cooked chops to a serving dish. Pour the sauce over them, garnish the chops with sautéed mushrooms and the fennel or dill leaves.

Serving suggestion
Best served with almond potatoes (page 132).

Freezing hint
If a large can of mango purée has been opened, and only half the quantity used, transfer the remaining purée into a plastic container and freeze it.

⊰⊱

Pork Chops Baked in Yogurt
Maans Chops Dahi Wali

The thick succulent pork chops are first sautéed in a frying pan and then baked in the oven. The chops are placed on pieces of foil, or banana leaves if you can get them, smothered in a mixture of tomatoes, onions and spices, then covered in natural yogurt, bundled up like a parcel and baked.

Serves 4
Preparation time: 25 minutes
Cooking time: 50–60minutes

4 large pork chops, each
   2.5cm/1 inch thick
1 tablespoon oil
2 medium onions
1 clove of garlic
2 medium tomatoes
1/2 teaspoon cumin seeds
1 1/2 teaspoons coriander
   powder

1 teaspoon salt
1/2 teaspoon chilli powder
4 large pieces of foil or
   banana leaves
8 tablespoons natural yogurt
2 tablespoons chopped fresh
   coriander leaves

1. Trim off the excess fat from the chops.
2. Wash them and pat them dry: if any moisture remains on the chops they will not brown properly.
3. Heat a frying pan, add the oil and place the chops in it. At first the chops will stick to the pan, but as soon as they release enough fat they will be easy to turn over. Brown the chops on both sides to a crisp golden brown. Remove and keep hot.
4. While the chops are cooking prepare the onions by chopping them finely. Crush the garlic. Scorch the tomatoes either by placing the tomatoes under a hot electric grill or by holding the tomato over a gas flame. (The best way is to insert a fork into the stalk end and then hold it over the flame.) As soon as the skin scorches and splits, the tomatoes also cook slightly. Remove the tomatoes and chop them finely.
5. Pour away all but one tablespoon of fat from the frying pan. Place it back on the heat and add the cumin seeds and onions. Stir-fry until transparent and soft, then add the crushed garlic. Stir-fry for another few minutes until a pale golden colour. Add the chopped tomatoes, coriander powder, salt and chilli powder. Stir-fry for a few minutes until the tomatoes are soft, and most of the moisture has dried up. Remove from the heat.
6. Lightly grease the pieces of foil or banana leaves. Place a chop in the centre, pile some tomato mixture on top and spread it all over the chop to cover it completely. Repeat this with all the chops and mixture.
7. Lightly whip the yogurt to a smooth consistency. Pour about 1¹/₂ tablespoons of yogurt on top of each chop. Then cover the chops with the foil or banana leaf, making sure it is completely covered. If banana leaves are used, secure them with some cocktail sticks.
8. Place the chops in an oval dish and cook in a slow oven – gas 2/150°C/300°F – for 50–60 minutes, until the chops are really tender. Serve sprinkled with freshly chopped coriander leaves.

Serving suggestion
This most delicious dish is best served with coriander rice (page 185) and whole stuffed sautéed courgettes (page 133).

Useful hint
Both the chops and the *masala*, i.e. the tomato and onion mixture, can be prepared well in advance and combined an hour before serving, giving time to cook through with the yogurt on top.

❦

Chilli Pork
Mirchi ka Maans

Aubergines and onions have always been dry-roasted to allow the skins to char before cooking. I find that chillies dry-roasted in the same way, i.e. over a naked flame until the skins are charred, then sweated for a few minutes in a polythene bag and peeled, produce a delicious flavour when used with other ingredients. It is best to use the short, fat variety of chilli for this dish.

Serves 4
Preparation time: 30 minutes
Cooking time: 25 minutes

3 green chillies
450g/1 lb pork fillet
Bunch of spring onions
1 unripe green mango
2–3 tablespoons oil

1½ teaspoons salt
1 teaspoon ground ajowan
2 tablespoons coarsely
 chopped fresh coriander
 leaves

1. Prepare the chillies by placing them on a wire mesh over a naked flame. Turning once or twice, completely allow the skin to char. Remove and place in a polythene bag, seal and leave to sweat for a few minutes. Remove from the bag and carefully peel off the skin, then remove the stalk and seeds. Roughly chop the chillies.
2. Cut the fillet into 2.5cm/1-inch pieces.
3. Cut the spring onions into 2.5cm/1-inch lengths.
4. Peel and coarsely grate the mango and discard its stone. (Reserve any juice.)
5. Heat the oil in a *karahi* or heavy-bottomed frying pan. Add the pork and stir-fry over high heat for a few minutes to seal in the juices.
6. Reduce the heat and continue stir-frying for another few minutes before adding the spring onions, chillies, mango and all the juice.
7. Stirring frequently, fry this mixture until the onions begin to soften.
8. Add the salt, ground ajowan and coriander leaves. Stir well.
9. Reduce the heat, cover and cook until the meat is really tender and the onions are soft but still crunchy.

Serving suggestion
Best served with hot nan (page 222) and an onion and lime juice salad (page 68).

Freezing hint
Cool quickly and place in freezer containers. Thaw completely before reheating.

Spicy Spinach Ham
Masaledar Palak Sooar Raan

A few Christmases ago some friends got together for a slap-up meal. They wanted a traditional European meal but with an Indian spicy flavour. Quite a tall order it seemed at that time, but the more I thought about it the more excited I became at the endless possibilities. My contribution to the dinner was the traditional ham stuffed with a spicy spinach mixture.

Serves 8–10
Preparation time: 40 minutes
Cooking time: 3½ hours

1 4kg/8–9 lb ham, fully cooked
450g/1 lb frozen or twice that amount of fresh spinach
2 tablespoons oil
2 medium onions, finely chopped
2.5cm/1-inch piece of fresh ginger, finely chopped
2 green chillies, finely chopped
1 clove of garlic, crushed
1 teaspoon salt
20 cloves
100g/4 oz clear honey
2 tablespoons lemon juice

1. Using a sharp knife, make very deep, criss-cross incisions into the ham. Place on a roasting dish.
2. Thoroughly wash the fresh spinach and chop it coarsely.
3. Heat the oil, add the onions and stir-fry until soft and transparent.
4. Add the ginger, green chillies and garlic. Stir-fry for a few more minutes until the onion is a golden colour.
5. Add the spinach, salt and about 150ml/¼ pint of water. Reduce the heat and leave to cook until the spinach is

tender and all the moisture has dried off. Leave until cool enough to handle.

6. Place the spinach in a food processor and purée to a smooth consistency.

7. Carefully open the ham incisions and stuff the spinach into them, using up all the spinach purée.

8. Using a skewer, make twenty holes in the ham's skin – ten holes on each side. Stick a clove into each hole.

9. Mix together the honey and lemon juice. Liberally coat this mixture over the ham. Place the ham in a preheated oven – gas 4/180°C/350°F – and cook for 2½–3 hours. Baste it frequently with the honey and lemon juice mixture. Turn the ham over once.

10. When the outside is crisp and golden and the inside thoroughly cooked, transfer the ham to a serving platter. Carve off some thick slices and serve.

Serving suggestion
Slices of spinach ham can be served on a bed of plain rice (page 184) and a tossed salad.

Freezing hint
Freeze in slices which will be easy to thaw before reheating.

Chicken Flavoured with Poppy Seeds
Murghi Rohani

A different approach to the marinating process, where instead of marinating the chicken in the spices and lemon juice, I have marinated only the spices in lemon juice and then poured the marinade over the sautéed chicken. The poppy seeds add a lovely nutty flavour to the chicken.

Serves 4
Preparation time: 25 minutes
Cooking time: 40 minutes

2.5cm/1-inch piece of fresh ginger
2 cloves of garlic
1 green chilli
225g/8 oz button onions or shallots
225g/8 oz button mushrooms
100g/4 oz ripe tomatoes
4 tablespoons lemon juice

¼ teaspoon chilli powder
½ teaspoon cinnamon powder
1¼ teaspoons salt
1 tablespoon poppy seeds
3 tablespoons oil
8 chicken pieces, skinned
2 tablespoons finely chopped coriander leaves

1. Peel and cut the ginger into thin slivers. Grind the garlic and green chilli.
2. Peel the shallots or button onions and keep them whole. Quickly wash the mushrooms, wipe dry, keep whole. Quarter, then halve the tomatoes.
3. In a bowl mix together the lemon juice, ground garlic and chilli, chilli powder, cinnamon, salt and poppy seeds.
4. Heat the oil and sauté the chicken pieces to a rich golden brown. Remove and keep warm.
5. Add the shallots and mushrooms and fry over high heat, stirring constantly, for about 5 minutes.
6. Replace the chicken pieces and continue frying for another few minutes.
7. Add the tomatoes and the marinated spices.
8. Continue frying over fairly high heat until the ingredients have blended well.
9. Reduce the heat and continue cooking until most of the moisture has evaporated and the chicken is really tender.
10. Sprinkle the coriander leaves on top and mix them into the rest of the ingredients. Remove from the heat and serve.

A delicious dish which I like serving with nan (page 222) and yogurt with roasted aubergines (page 206).

❦

Chicken and Coriander Leaves in Lemon Juice
Murghi Dhania ka Milan

Coriander plays a very important part in Indian food, the seeds as a spice and the leaves and stems as a herb. A highly aromatic and somewhat pungent herb, it combines very well with most flavours, either as the main flavouring herb, as in the case of this dish, or as a garnish to a host of others.

Serves 4
Preparation time: 30 minutes plus 6–8 hours marinating
Cooking time: 35–45 minutes

1 1–1½kg/2½–3 lb chicken
2 large bunches of fresh
   coriander leaves
2 cloves of garlic
5cm/2-inch piece of fresh
   ginger
Juice of 2 lemons
½ teaspoon garam masala

1 teaspoon paprika
½ teaspoon chilli powder
1 teaspoon black cumin
   seeds
1 teaspoon salt
2–3 tablespoons ghee or oil
5 fresh ripe tomatoes

1. Divide the chicken into 8 portions (the carcase can be used to make soup or stock).
2. Coarsely chop the fresh coriander leaves, crush the garlic and finely slice the ginger. Mix together all the ingredients except the chicken, ghee and the tomatoes.
3. Add the chicken pieces to the marinade and leave it in the refrigerator for 6–8 hours. Baste the pieces a few times to ensure that the marinade soaks through the chicken.

4. Heat the ghee or oil and when hot add the chicken and the marinade. Increase the heat and let the chicken brown evenly to a golden colour. At this stage most of the lemon juice and any additional moisture will have evaporated.
5. Stir-fry the chicken for another few minutes. Finely chop the tomatoes, leaving the skins on. Add these to the chicken, stir-fry for a few minutes, then cover and cook for a further 10 minutes on low heat until the tomatoes are reduced to a pulp. Serve piping hot.

Serving suggestion
I find this an excellent aromatic dish for serving on warm summer days. Best served with tossed green salad and either nan (page 222) or shop-bought Greek pitta.

Freezing hint
This dish can be frozen easily either with the marinade in its uncooked state, or can be cooked and then frozen. It is important to thaw out the chicken completely before reheating.

❦

Honey Chicken
Shaihad ke Murghi

Honey combines very well with lemon juice, and in this recipe the only spice that I have added is ajowan, for which the only substitute I can recommend is fresh thyme. The ajowan is first quickly fried in hot oil and then added to the honey and lemon juice mixture.

Serves 4
Preparation time: 20 minutes plus 3 hours marinating
Cooking time: 45 minutes

4 chicken quarters
175g/6 oz clear honey
150ml/¹/₄ pint fresh lemon
  juice
1¹/₂ teaspoons salt

1 teaspoon freshly ground
  black pepper
1 tablespoon oil
¹/₂ tablespoon ajowan seeds

1. Skin the chicken quarters. With a sharp knife, make one or two incisions on the chicken pieces.
2. Mix together the honey, lemon juice, salt and black pepper.
3. Heat the oil, add the ajowan seeds and, as soon as they pop, pour the seeds on to the honey and lemon juice mixture. Stir well to mix all the ingredients.
4. Pour this mixture over the chicken quarters and leave to marinate for at least 3 hours.
5. Preheat the oven to gas 3/170°C/325°F, place the marinated chicken in the oven and, basting frequently, cook for 45 minutes until the chicken is a rich golden colour and really tender. Turn the chicken pieces once.

Serving suggestion
Serve hot with plain boiled rice and stuffed whole cauliflower (page 135). Alternatively serve with almond potatoes (page 132) and a tossed salad.

Sesame Baked Chicken
Murghi Til Wali

Sesame seed, a native of India, is one of the most important oil seeds in the world. The subtle nutty flavour of the seed is enhanced after slight roasting. Usually scattered over breads and cakes in the West, it is used as a paste and its oil as a cooking medium in the East. The oil is colourless, odourless and light.

Serves 4
Preparation time: 25 minutes plus 1¹/₂ hours marinating
Cooking time: 30–35 minutes

1 1kg/2-lb chicken cut into 8 pieces
4 tablespoons lemon juice
1¹/₂ tablespoons finely minced ginger
1 clove of garlic, crushed

1 tablespoon sesame seed oil
1¹/₂ teaspoons salt
¹/₂ teaspoon chilli powder
¹/₂ teaspoon allspice
3 tablespoons sesame seeds

1. Remove the skin from the chicken pieces and, using a sharp knife, make deep cuts into the meat.
2. Mix together all the ingredients except the sesame seeds.
3. Add the chicken pieces to the marinade, cover and leave to marinate for 1¹/₂ hours. Turn the chicken pieces once or twice to keep them well covered and moist.
4. Remove from the marinade (but reserve the marinade).
5. Place the sesame seeds on a flat dish and thoroughly coat the chicken pieces with them.
6. Preheat the oven to gas 4/180°C/350°F.
7. Place the sesame-coated chicken on a shallow ovenproof dish, making sure that the chicken pieces do not overlap one another.
8. Cook for 25–30 minutes until the chicken is tender.
9. In the meantime, pour the marinade into a saucepan and bring it to the boil, reduce the heat and simmer gently for 5 minutes to thicken. Serve hot as an accompanying sauce for the chicken.

Serving suggestion
Serve hot with plain nan (page 222) and tossed green and spring onion salad accompanied by the thickened sauce. Or eat cold with a tossed salad.

Freezing hint
Freeze in individual portions. Thaw and reheat thoroughly before serving.

Chicken Stuffed with Peppers
Murghi Bari Mirch ke Saath

Chicken, being a fairly bland meat, goes well with almost any combination of other ingredients. In this particular dish I have stuffed chicken breasts with a mixture of spiced peppers, rolled up the breasts and sautéed them in oil, or covered and baked.

Serves 4
Preparation time: 30 minutes
Cooking time: 40 minutes

1 large green pepper
1 large red pepper
4 tablespoons oil
1 teaspoon cumin seeds
1 medium onion, peeled and
   finely chopped

1 clove of garlic, crushed
3/4 teaspoon salt
1/2 teaspoon chilli powder
1 ripe tomato, peeled and
   chopped
4 chicken breasts, skinned

1. Remove the stalks, seeds and any white pith from both the peppers. Cut them into very small pieces.
2. Heat 1½ tablespoons of the oil in a frying pan. Add the cumin seeds and, as soon as they pop and splutter, add the chopped onion.
3. Stir-fry to a rich golden colour, then add the chopped red and green peppers, garlic, salt and chilli powder.
4. Fry for a few minutes then add the chopped tomato. Stir well and cook over moderate heat, stirring frequently, until the peppers are cooked but not too soft and all the moisture from the tomato has evaporated. Put aside until cool enough to handle easily. Wash the pan.
5. Flatten the chicken breasts with a wooden meat hammer.
6. Divide the pepper mixture into 4 portions. Spread it all

over each chicken breast then roll each one up tightly. Wind a length of cotton thread around each chicken roll, so that they do not open up during frying or baking.

7. If the chicken breasts are to be sautéed, heat the remaining oil in the frying pan. Add the chicken breasts and sauté gently, turning once, until a rich golden colour.

8. If the chicken breasts are to be baked in the oven, lightly grease a shallow oven dish, place the chicken rolls in it, glaze the breasts with a little oil, cover and bake in a warm oven – gas 4/180°C/350°F – for 25 minutes until the breast is cooked.

9. Remove the chicken rolls from the frying pan or oven, undo the cotton thread and cut each roll into 1cm/^{1}/$_2$-inch thick slices.

10. Arrange on individual serving dishes, surrounded by shredded lettuce.

Serving suggestion
Serve hot, cut in thick slices as an appetizer with drinks or as a starter, or as the main dish.

Freezing hint
Can be frozen cooked or uncooked. Thaw completely before reheating.

∝◦⊲

Green Herb Chicken
Chicken Amar

The subtle combination of green coriander, green spring onions and green peppers is extremely exciting. As very little fat is used for the cooking, this makes an ideal dish for figure-conscious people.

Serves 4
Preparation time: 25 minutes
Cooking time: 25–30 minutes

8 chicken thighs
2 medium-sized green
  peppers
8–10 green spring onions
1–2 fresh green chillies

25g/1 oz fresh green ginger
2–3 tablespoons oil
50g/2 oz freshly chopped
  green coriander leaves
1¼ teaspoons salt

1. Skin the thighs, then keep them covered while preparing the vegetables.
2. Remove the stalks, seeds and pith from the green peppers and cut them into 0.5cm/¼-inch thin strips.
3. Remove the bulb ends and any shrivelled-up green leaves from the onions and cut them into 2.5cm/1-inch long pieces.
4. Remove the stalk and finely chop the green chilli.
5. Scrape the skin from the ginger and cut into thin julienne strips.
6. Heat the oil in a *karahi*, add the skinned chicken and stir-fry to a golden colour.
7. Add all the ingredients and the salt and, stirring frequently, cook for a further 10 minutes until the peppers are cooked but still crisp.

Serving suggestion
Serve hot with chappati (page 211) and spinach in yogurt (page 203).

✎◦✎

Roast Aubergine and Chicken
Baingan aur Murghi ka Bhartha

The birth of this truly delicious dish happened on a cold winter night in Delhi. Relaxing with friends, I suddenly asked them if there was any chicken in the house. The time was quite late, but having got the idea I just had to try it out. A chicken was brought and I set about trying a variation on the classic Punjabi dish of aubergine *bhartha*, in which an aubergine is roasted over a naked flame and then cooked in a combination of tomatoes, onions, spices and herbs.

Serves 4
Preparation time: 1½ hours
Cooking time: 20 minutes

2 chicken breasts
600ml/1 pint water
2.5cm/1-inch piece of fresh
  ginger
1 clove of garlic
3 cloves
2.5cm/1-inch piece of
  cinnamon
6 whole black peppercorns
1 black cardamom

1 bay leaf
1 large round aubergine
2 medium onions
3–4 fresh tomatoes
1–2 green chillies (optional)
2 tablespoons oil
1 teaspoon salt
½ teaspoon chilli powder
1 tablespoon freshly
  chopped coriander leaves

1. Wash the chicken, remove its skin, place in the saucepan and cover with the water.
2. Coarsely chop the ginger and garlic. Place in a piece of muslin along with the cinnamon, peppercorns, cardamom and bay leaf and tie them up.
3. Add this bouquet garni to the chicken. Bring it to the boil, reduce the heat and leave to simmer. Carefully remove any scum that may appear on the surface.
4. Leave to simmer gently for about 1 hour until the chicken is really tender. Remove the bouquet garni and reserve the stock (it can be used for soup or stock and can be frozen).
5. Chop the chicken into small pieces.
6. While the chicken is cooking, roast the aubergine over a naked flame until all the skin is charred.
7. Remove from the flame and carefully peel off the charred skin. Discard the stalk and roughly chop the aubergine.
8. Peel and finely chop the onions, tomatoes and chillies.
9. Heat the oil in a heavy-bottomed frying pan or *karahi*.

10. Add the onions and, stirring frequently, fry until they turn a pale golden colour.
11. Add the chicken and aubergine. Again stirring frequently, fry until they are well mixed.
12. Finally, add the tomatoes, green chillies, salt and chilli powder. Mix well.
13. Reduce the heat, cover and cook for 10–15 minutes until the ingredients are well blended, the tomatoes have reduced to a pulp and the oil begins to separate.
14. Serve hot, sprinkled with the coriander leaves.

Serving suggestion
An excellent accompaniment to a main meal consisting of baked channa dal (page 116), yogurt (page 47) and chappatis (page 211).

Freezing hint
Excellent for freezing. Thaw, reheat and sprinkle with freshly chopped coriander leaves.

⊲⊏◦⊐⊳

Chicken Marinated in Pomegranate Seeds and Juices
Anardane ki Murghi

The delicate flavour and aroma of pomegranate juice is very rarely used in cooking. In this dish I have combined the pomegranate juice and the dried seeds to impart a unique flavour.

Serves 4
Preparation time: 20 minutes plus 4–5 hours marinating
Cooking time: 40 minutes

4 tablespoons dried
  pomegranate seeds
Juice of 2 pomegranates
1¹/₂ teaspoons garam masala
Salt to taste

Freshly ground black pepper
  to taste
8 chicken drumsticks
2 tablespoons ghee
Fresh green coriander leaves

1. Pomegranate juice is now available at good Indian grocers, but if fresh pomegranates are used, then deseed them by gently prising them free from the shell. Remove all the white pith which is bitter. Place the juicy seeds in a blender and blend them for a few seconds, then strain through a medium-sized sieve. Reserve the juice and throw away the seeds.

2. Dry pomegranate seeds have the juicy flesh sticking to them. It is this flesh that gives the tang and flavour. Wash the seeds gently, taking care not to scrape off any of the pulp. Place them in the blender with a little of the juice and blend to a smooth paste. The seeds won't liquidize completely as they are very hard, but this gives the dish a crunchy texture.

3. Mix all the juice, the purée, garam masala, salt and black pepper in a bowl.

4. Remove the skin from the drumsticks and lightly prick them with the point of a sharp knife. Place them in an ovenproof dish and pour the pomegranate purée on top, making sure that all the pieces are thoroughly covered.

5. Leave to marinate for 4–5 hours, turning the chicken occasionally to let the marinade seep in from all sides.

6. Preheat an oven to gas 3/170°C/325°F. Melt the ghee and pour it on top of the chicken. Place the dish into the oven and cook it uncovered for about 40 minutes until the chicken is tender and the pomegranate purée has formed a crunchy crust on top.

7. Serve sprinkled with freshly chopped coriander leaves.

Serving suggestion
An excellent dish to be enjoyed hot or cold. I find it a great success on picnics when served with some fresh tossed green salad, onion and tomato salad and wedges of lemon, with some spicy mint and yogurt chutney (page 252).

Freezing hint
I find that this dish can easily be frozen either cooked or uncooked. If it is to be frozen uncooked, then proceed up to the marinade stage and freeze it either in a container or plastic bag. If frozen cooked, then cool it down quickly and freeze it. In both cases, it is important to thaw the dish completely before cooking or eating.

❦

Peppers, Chicken and Fresh Ginger
Pahari Mirch aur Murghi

Over the last few years peppers of various colours and sizes have become more readily available in greengrocers, and I find people are becoming more adventurous in trying out this delicious vegetable. Apart from the usual green and red peppers, pale orange, yellow and even purple-coloured ones are appearing on the market. Fresh ginger, also now easily available, makes an interesting combination with the peppers.

Serves 4
Preparation time: 20 minutes
Cooking time: 25 minutes

2 chicken breasts	3 tablespoons oil
2 red peppers	½ teaspoon ground cloves
2 orange peppers	½ teaspoon ground
2 green peppers	cinnamon
2 cloves of garlic	½ teaspoon chilli powder
5cm/2-inch piece of fresh	1½ teaspoons salt
green ginger	

1. Cut the chicken breast into 5cm/2-inch pieces.
2. Quarter all the peppers, discarding the stalks and seeds. Cut them into half again.
3. Peel the garlic cloves and crush them. Peel the ginger and cut it into fine strips.
4. Heat the oil in a frying pan, add the chicken pieces and stir-fry until golden in colour.
5. Add the peppers, ginger and garlic. Stirring frequently, fry for a few minutes until the peppers begin to soften.
6. Add the three ground spices and salt. Stir well to mix the ingredients.
7. Reduce the heat, cover and cook until the chicken is tender. Serve hot.

Serving suggestion
Serve with plain rice (page 184) and plain yogurt (page 47) or with almond potatoes (page 132).

Freezing hint
Freezes very well. Remember to thaw out completely before reheating.

⬤▭◦⊏▭

Stuffed Cornish Hens
Chooti Murghi Bhari hui

Another exciting combination in which spices are stuffed

between the flesh and the skin of the bird and the cavity is stuffed with a delightful mixture of fruits such as apples, apricots, prunes and raisins. This bird is then trussed and baked in the oven. Half a Cornish hen with the stuffing is enough per person.

Serves 6
Preparation time: 40 minutes
Cooking time: 1³/₄ hours

50g/2 oz raisins
1 medium onion
2 medium-sized green apples
225g/8 oz dried apricots
225g/8 oz stoned prunes
50g/2 oz butter

Small pinch of ground cinnamon
¹/₂ teaspoon freshly ground black pepper
³/₄ teaspoon salt
3 Cornish hens or poussins

Spices
2 tablespoons coriander seeds
¹/₂ teaspoon black peppercorns
Small pinch of ground cloves

Small pinch of ground cardamom
¹/₂ teaspoon salt
2 tablespoons ghee

1. Soak the raisins for about 20 minutes. Drain them and squeeze out excess water.
2. Peel and finely chop the onion, and peel, core and chop the apples. Chop the apricots and prunes into small pieces.
3. Heat the butter and sauté the onions to a pale golden brown. Add the fruits, cinnamon, black pepper and salt, continue sautéing the mixture for another 10 minutes, stirring frequently until the mixture is soft. Put aside to cool.
4. Grind the coriander seeds and black peppercorns to a fine powder. Mix all the rest of the spices with the ghee.
5. Very carefully separate the delicate skin from the hens' flesh. (To do this you will have to slide your finger gently

in between the skin and flesh and carefully separate it all
around the bird, as far as possible.)

6. Insert a little of the spice mixture at a time and carefully
   spread it between the skin and flesh.
7. Stuff the cavities with the fruit mixture, truss the hens and
   place them in a deep ovenproof dish.
8. Cover and roast in a preheated oven – gas 5/190°C/375°F
   – for 1½ hours.
9. Halfway through, turn the hens over to roast on their
   other sides.
10. Remove from the casserole and, using sharp kitchen
    scissors, cut each hen in half.

Serving suggestion
Serve hot with coriander rice (page 185) to enhance the strong
flavour of the coriander in the stuffing.

Freezing hint
Can be frozen successfully, but I would cut them in half first,
wrap each half individually in freezer cling-film or foil. Thaw
out completely before reheating.

❧

Duck Stuffed with Spicy Dates
Khajoor Bhari Batak

Duck to most people represents a dish that has little meat but
a lot of fat and apart from currying it or roasting it in orange
juice, very little else is done with it. In this dish I have stuffed
the duck with some spicy stoneless dates and then baked it with
fresh orange juice and lightly crushed aniseed.

Serves 4
Preparation time: 35 minutes
Cooking time: 1½ hours

116

1 medium-sized duck
300ml/½ pint fresh orange
  juice
2 tablespoons lightly crushed
  aniseed

1 teaspoon salt
½ teaspoon freshly ground
  black pepper

Stuffing
225g/8 oz stoned dates,
  coarsely chopped
1 teaspoon ground cumin
1 teaspoon ground coriander

1 teaspoon chilli powder
1 teaspoon garam masala
½ teaspoon salt

1. If you are using a frozen duck, make sure it is completely thawed before cooking. Remove the giblet packet from inside the cavity. (If it is a prepared bird, it is probably bought trussed. If bought from a farm, you will need to truss it before stuffing.)
2. In a bowl mix together the chopped dates and the stuffing spices and salt.
3. Carefully lift up the skin at the neck end of the duck. Stuff the cavity with the chopped date mixture. Close the skin over the hole and secure with a cocktail stick. Place the duck in a roasting dish.
4. Using a sharp knife, make a few deep incisions on the skin all over the duck.
5. Mix together the fresh orange juice, aniseed, salt and black pepper.
6. Pour this mixture over the stuffed duck and cook in a low oven – gas 3/170°C/325°F – for 1½ hours. Remember to baste regularly. Turn the duck once during cooking.
7. Remove from the roasting dish, undo the trussing and serve neatly carved with the stuffing. Serve the sauce separately.

Serving suggestion
Serve this duck with plain boiled rice and a nice tossed green salad.

Fish and Shellfish

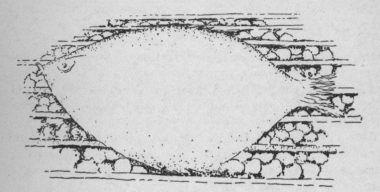

With a coastline as fabulous as that of India, and with its large flowing rivers, fish and shellfish are plentiful: giant crabs, prawns, fresh pomfrets and hilsa fish are found in abundance. Fortunately most Indian fishes can be replaced by fish bought in the West.

Fish cookery along the coast of India differs from region to region because of the availability of local spices and other ingredients, e.g., plenty of coconut milk and fresh grated coconut are used in the west, tamarind in the south, mustard oil and seeds in the east, rich onion-based sauces in the north.

In this chapter I have used the traditional ingredients but changed the method of cooking. Fish is often wrapped in banana leaves and then shallow-fried; but as fresh banana leaves are not available in Britain, I have enclosed the fish in a spicy coconut chutney, then wrapped it in foil and baked it in the oven.

Some specialist grocery shops do now import green or yellow unripe coconuts, so what could be more delicious than giant prawns that have been lightly spiced and mixed with the soft white coconut flesh, the top sealed and the whole coconut baked in the oven or surrounded by live charcoal.

The delicate flavour of fish and shellfish is often lost due to overspicing and overcooking, therefore the emphasis in this chapter is on the subtle combination of spices and complementary ingredients. The recipes have been created for the purpose of being served on their own or with salad, rice or chappatis, but no other accompaniments are required.

Although only a limited variety of fish are mentioned, there is no reason why appropriate alternatives cannot be used. These recipes are meant to fire your own imagination as much as to be used as basic recipes.

Steamed Whole Fish
Bhap di hui Machchi

A superb steamed fish without any excessive added flavouring. The crucial element of this dish is the spray of hot oil sprinkled on top, which improves the appearance.

Serves 4
Preparation time: 20 minutes
Cooking time: 15–20 minutes

119

1 sea bass, white fish or
   trout, about 1kg/2 lbs
Small bunch of fresh dill
2.5cm/1-inch piece of fresh
   ginger

2 large onions
Juice of 1 lemon
$^1/_2$ teaspoon salt
Freshly ground black pepper
2 tablespoons oil

1. Have the fish cleaned and scaled, but leave the head and tail on because this helps to preserve the flavour and, of course, makes the fish look more attractive. Rinse and dry it thoroughly. With the point of a sharp knife make 3 diagonal slashes, 2.5cm/1 inch apart, on each side of the fish. This helps the fish to cook evenly.

2. Place the fish on a heatproof platter. Coarsely chop the dill, peel and finely shred the ginger. Finely slice the onions.

3. Mix together the lemon juice, salt, dill, ginger and black pepper. Rub this mixture over and inside the fish, making sure that the ginger is evenly distributed.

4. Prepare a fish steamer. If an improvised steamer is used, make sure it is stable. If a roasting pan is used, place a suitable rack in it. Pour boiling water into the pan to reach 2.5cm/1 inch below the rack. Return the water to the boil, then lower the heat to simmering and place the platter containing the fish on the rack. Cover and slightly increase the heat so that the water is simmering fast.

5. Steam the fish for about 15 minutes, adding more boiling water if necessary. When the fish is cooked, the eyes will be white and the tip of a knife will come away clean when inserted into the thickest part of the fish.

6. Remove the platter from the pot and transfer the fish to a serving dish. Sprinkle the finely sliced onions on top.

7. Heat the oil in a small pan, taking care not to let it smoke. Pour this hot oil over the fish and onions and serve at once.

Serving suggestion
Excellent as a fish course with a yogurt chutney (page 252), or even as a starter, in which case this quantity would serve 8.

Crunchy Cod in Coconut
Machchi Lajawab Nariyal ki

The soft flesh of fish marries well with the crunchy coconut and sesame seeds. Thinly pared lemon rind adds just the right amount of colour to the end product. The subtle flavour of the coconut milk is enhanced by the addition of lemon juice and sautéed onions. Any other white fish can be used instead of cod steaks. It is best to ask the fishmonger to cut the steaks to a thickness of 3.5cm/1½ inches.

Serves 4
Preparation time: 25 minutes
Cooking time: 30 minutes

4 3.5cm/1½-inch thick cod
  steaks
2 medium onions
100g/4 oz button
  mushrooms
Rind of 1 lemon
2 tablespoons oil

1 teaspoon mustard seeds
¾ teaspoon salt
¼ teaspoon chilli powder
300ml/½ pint thick coconut
  milk
25g/1 oz desiccated coconut
1 tablespoon sesame seeds

1. Carefully wash the cod steaks and pat them dry with kitchen paper.
2. Cut the onions into 0.5cm/¼-inch thick rings and separate them. Finely slice the mushrooms. Remove the white pith from the lemon rind and cut it into 2.5cm/1-inch long, very thin strips.
3. Heat the oil, add the mustard seeds and, as soon as they pop, add the onion rings and sauté to a light golden colour.
4. Add the mushrooms and carry on sautéing for another few minutes.

121

5. Add the salt and chilli powder and pour in the coconut milk. Stir well and bring to simmering point.
6. Gently place the cod steaks in the sauce, spoon some liquid over them, cover and cook for about 20 minutes over a very low heat.
7. Spread the desiccated coconut and sesame seeds on a grill pan and toast lightly to a golden brown.
8. Carefully lift the cooked fish on to a serving dish and spoon some of the coconut sauce over each steak. Sprinkle the lightly toasted coconut and sesame seeds on top, then a few strips of lemon rind, and serve at once.

Serving suggestion
Serve hot as a fish course or as part of the main meal. If smaller portions of fish are used, then serve as a starter.

⋐⊙⋑

Pomfret and Coconut Delight
Pomfret aur Nariyal ka Maza

Pomfret is definitely the most popular of the flat fishes along the western coast of India. Although it is available in Britain only at specialist shops, you can use sole or plaice as a substitute. For the stuffing I have used a spicy coriander chutney, then I've poached the fish in coconut milk.

Serves 4
Preparation time: 30 minutes
Cooking time: 35–40 minutes

4 small pomfrets, sole or plaice
300ml/^{1}/$_2$ pint thick coconut milk (see page 49)

1 teaspoon salt
^{1}/$_4$ teaspoon chilli powder
1 tablespoon oil
1^1/$_2$ teaspoons mustard seeds

122

Coriander chutney

1 small bunch of coriander leaves	1 green chilli
1 medium onion	3–4 tablespoons lemon juice
1 clove of garlic	$^1/_2$ teaspoon salt

1. Descale and clean the fish. Leave heads and tails intact if preferred, otherwise cut them off. Wash thoroughly.
2. Using a sharp knife, make three deep incisions on either side of the fish.
3. Next, prepare the coriander chutney. Cut off the very coarse stalks from the coriander, skin and roughly chop the onion and garlic and cut off the green chilli's stalk. Place these ingredients and the lemon juice and salt in a food processor and purée to a smooth consistency.
4. Carefully open up the cavity in the fish and stuff some of the chutney inside, also in the incisions on both sides. Place the fish flat in an ovenproof dish, making sure that they do not overlap.
5. Mix the coconut milk, salt and chilli powder in a bowl.
6. Heat the oil, add the mustard seeds and as soon as they pop pour them over the coconut milk, mix well, then pour this mixture over the fish, making sure that the coconut milk also seeps under the fish.
7. Bake in a hot oven – gas 5/190°C/375°F – for 25 minutes until the fish is tender. Remember to baste from time to time.
8. Remove and serve hot at once.

Serving suggestion

Serve as a separate course with a fresh green salad, or as part of the main meal where no meat or poultry is being served.

Freezing hint

If fresh fish has been used then proceed up to the stuffing stage. Wrap each fish in freezer paper and freeze. Thaw out completely and cook.

Fish in Yogurt and Saffron Sauce
Dahi Machchi Kesar Wali

In certain parts of India there is a superstition that yogurt or any milk product should not be eaten with fish. I have never been able to discover the reason behind this, but no doubt someone will tell me one fine day. The delicate flavour of saffron enhances the yogurt and red pepper sauce.

Serves 4
Preparation time: 30 minutes
Cooking time: 25 minutes

4 small pomfrets, sole or plaice
1 red pimento
300ml/¹/₂ pint natural yogurt
1 teaspoon cornflour
Large pinch of saffron
³/₄ teaspoon salt
¹/₂ teaspoon chilli powder

1. Skin and fillet the fish. Pat dry.
2. Cut the pimento into quarters and remove the white pith, seeds and stalk. Cut into small pieces.
3. Lightly whip the yogurt to a smooth consistency. Add the cornflour and whisk it in until no lumps remain.
4. Pour the yogurt mixture into a sauté pan and, stirring continuously, bring it to the boil. This will thicken the sauce.
5. Add the saffron, salt, chilli powder and pimento. Stir well and cook for another minute.
6. Carefully add the fillets, cover with sauce and allow to cook for 10 minutes at a very low heat.

Serving suggestion
Serve hot as a separate course or lightly chilled as a starter.

Fish and Tomato Mixture
Machchi ka Bhartha

Bhartha is a very traditional dish, usually made of vegetables such as aubergines which are roasted over a naked flame, skinned and sautéed in a mixture of tomatoes and onions. Using the same principle, I have made fish *bhartha*, where I grill the fish under a hot grill or over charcoal, skin and bone it, then use the flaked flesh in the same onion and tomato mixture.

Serves 4
Preparation time: 20 minutes
Cooking time: 30–35 minutes

2 pomfrets, sole or plaice
2 medium onions
Small piece of fresh ginger
1 clove of garlic
1 green chilli
2 large tomatoes
Small bunch of coriander
 leaves
2 tablespoons oil
1/2 teaspoon cumin seeds
1 teaspoon salt
1/4 teaspoon turmeric

1. Thoroughly wash and pat dry the fish. Place under a hot grill or over live charcoal and cook until the skin is really charred. Remove from the heat and carefully remove the skin.
2. Using a fork, carefully remove all the cooked flesh and break it up into small flakes.
3. Finely chop the onions. Grind together the ginger, garlic and green chilli. Skin the tomatoes, remove their seeds and chop up finely. Finely chop the coriander leaves.
4. Heat the oil, add the cumin seeds and, as soon as they pop, add the onions and sauté to a pale golden colour.
5. Add the ginger, garlic and green chilli mixture. Stir-fry for

another few minutes then add the tomatoes, salt and turmeric.

6. Stirring frequently, cook this mixture until the tomatoes go really soft. (Add a couple of tablespoons of water if the mixture sticks to the bottom of the pan.)
7. Add the flaked fish and coriander leaves. Stir well, cover with a tight-fitting lid, reduce the heat and cook for about 10 minutes, stirring once or twice.

Serving suggestion
Serve hot as part of the main meal with other accompaniments or as a separate fish course with a ring of rice or a small chappati (page 211).

❧⚬❧

Tamarind Fish
Machchi Imli ke Saath

Cod steaks cooked in tamarind sauce adds a new dimension to the fish. The sauce is further enhanced by using aniseed and black peppercorns.

Serves 4
Preparation time: 30 minutes
Cooking time: 25 minutes

675g/1¹/₂ lbs cod
1 clove of garlic
1 green chilli
1 medium onion
1 tablespoon aniseeds
8 whole black peppercorns
50g/2 oz tamarind or 2
   tablespoons tamarind
   concentrate

1¹/₂ tablespoons sugar
1¹/₄ teaspoons salt
1 tablespoon oil
Small bunch of coriander
   leaves, finely chopped

1. Skin the fish and cut it into large chunks. Wash and dry thoroughly.
2. Grind the garlic, green chilli and onion into a fine paste.
3. Lightly crush the aniseed and black peppercorns.
4. If tamarind concentrate is being used, dilute it to 300ml/^{1}/$_2$ pint with water. If the slab is used, soak the 50g/2 oz tamarind in 300ml/^{1}/$_2$ pint warm water for about 20 minutes. With your fingers, loosen all the pulp and strain through a sieve, pressing down the warm pulp to the sides of the sieve. Discard the fibres, skin and any pips. Use the strained juice.
5. Add the sugar, aniseeds, black pepper and salt to the tamarind juice. Stir well to dissolve the sugar. (Do taste it at this stage in case you find the tamarind juice too sharp. Adjust the seasoning.)
6. Heat the oil, add the onion mixture and, stirring frequently, sauté the mixture for a few minutes until it turns a pale golden colour.
7. Pour in the tamarind juice and stir to blend all the ingredients. Reduce the heat and, stirring frequently, bring the mixture to the boil, then allow to simmer gently for a few minutes.
8. Carefully add the fish, cover with the sauce and cook for about 10 minutes, turning once, until the fish is tender and has absorbed some of the sauce.
9. Transfer to a serving dish and sprinkle finely chopped coriander leaves on top.

Serving suggestion
Serve hot as part of the main meal along with plain boiled rice and a simple dal preparation. Serve cold as a starter or as a fish course with a small amount of plain boiled rice.

Spicy Prawns
Coated with Sesame Seeds
Til Jhinga Masaladar

All along the coast of India delicious, king-size prawns are available in abundance. If large fresh prawns are not available then use frozen ones. The crunchy sesame seed coating on the outside enhances the softness of the prawns.

Serves 4
Preparation time: 25 minutes plus 30 minutes marinating
Cooking time: 15 minutes

16 large precooked fresh prawns or 225g/8 oz large frozen prawns
2 tablespoons lemon juice
1 teaspoon salt
1/2 teaspoon chilli powder
2 eggs
50g/2 oz sesame seeds
Lemon wedges
A few sprigs of fresh coriander leaves, washed

1. If fresh prawns are used, shell, top and devein them. If frozen prawns are used, thaw completely and dry on kitchen paper.
2. Mix together the lemon juice, salt and chilli powder. Pour this over the prawns and leave them to marinate for at least 30 minutes.
3. Lightly beat the eggs in a shallow dish.
4. In another shallow dish, spread the sesame seeds.
5. Carefully lift the prawns one at a time from the marinade and dip each one first into the egg and then into the sesame seeds, so that the prawns are completely covered by the seeds.
6. Place these prawns in a shallow ovenproof dish and bake

at gas 4/180°C/350°F for 15–20 minutes until the sesame seeds are browned.

7. Serve at once with lemon wedges and coriander sprigs.

Serving suggestion
Serve as a starter or appetizer with drinks, or as a fish course.

⊷∘⊶

Spicy Baked Prawns
Masale Wale Jhinge

The largest prawns give the best flavour to this dish, in which shelled and cleaned prawns are marinated in a subtly spiced sauce, then baked.

Serves 4
Preparation time: 10 minutes plus 2–3 hours marinating
Cooking time: 30–40 minutes

450g/1 lb fresh king-size prawns or 8–10 frozen king-sized prawns
2 medium onions
2.5cm/1-inch piece of fresh ginger
1 clove of garlic
1 1/2 teaspoons coarsely ground aniseeds

2 tablespoons desiccated coconut
1/2 teaspoon chilli powder
1 teaspoon salt
Freshly ground black pepper
150ml/1/4 pint coconut milk
1 tablespoon ghee
Freshly chopped green coriander leaves

1. If fresh prawns are used, clean them thoroughly, top and tail and devein them. If frozen prawns are used, completely thaw them and gently squeeze out any moisture.

2. Peel and finely grind the onions, ginger and garlic into a smooth paste. Place the mixture in a bowl with the

129

aniseeds, coconut, chilli powder, salt, black pepper and coconut milk. Mix these ingredients together in an ovenproof dish.

3. Add the prawns, stirring to cover completely. Leave to marinate in the refrigerator for 2–3 hours.
4. Preheat the oven to gas 3/170°C/325°F. Melt the ghee and pour it into the marinade. Cover the dish, place it in the oven and let it cook until nearly done (about 30 minutes). Remember to baste frequently so that the prawns do not dry out.
5. Uncover the dish for the last 10 minutes of the cooking time to allow a crisp crust to form on top.
6. Serve at once, sprinkled with the coriander.

Serving suggestion
This also forms an excellent starter to a main meal, in which case I like to serve it with thin slices of toast. Two or three prawns per head would be sufficient when served as a starter, but of course it is also an excellent main course.

Vegetables

In this chapter I want to introduce new and exciting variations into the ways of cooking both the common and the more exotic vegetables which can then be served either as an appropriate accompaniment to the main meal or as an excellent separate dish with just rice or chappati, or even on its own as a starter – for example, large aubergines stuffed with mushy green peas, or stuffed tomatoes with eggs, or bitter gourd cooked with tomatoes. None of the recipes includes a sauce, because I like my humble or exotic vegetable to show its true colour and be recognized for what it is, not masked in a sauce.

Vegetables such as cauliflower which is available throughout the year in the West are a seasonal and sometimes expensive vegetable in the East. Aubergines which are still considered exotic in the West are treated quite humbly in the East. With this in mind, I have selected a cross-section of vegetables.

⬥

New Potatoes and Almonds in Dry Spices
Badam Wale Aaloo

The unique soft and crunchy texture of this dish makes it one of my favourites. New potatoes add their own subtle flavour, although old potatoes can also be used, in which case select the smallest ones that you can find.

Serves 4
Preparation time: 20 minutes
Cooking time: 20 minutes

450g/1 lb new potatoes
50g/2 oz almond slivers
2 tablespoons oil
1 1/2 teaspoons cumin seeds
2 tablespoons ground
  coriander

1 tablespoon dried mint
1 teaspoon salt
1/2 teaspoon chilli powder

1. Thoroughly wash and scrub the new potatoes. Boil them in a little salted water until tender. Don't let them split open. If old potatoes have been used, peel after boiling and allowing them to cool.
2. Although this is the most time-consuming process it is well worth the effort: one by one, poke the almond slivers into the boiled potatoes, leaving about 3mm/1/8 inch uncovered at the surface.
3. Heat the oil in a heavy-bottomed frying pan. Add the cumin seeds and, as soon as they pop, add the coriander, mint, salt and chilli powder. Stir-fry for a second or two.

132

4. Add the prepared potatoes and stir-fry for a few minutes so that the fried spices have a chance to stick to the boiled potatoes and thus form a crusty coating on the potatoes.

Serving suggestion
A most versatile dish which can be eaten either hot or cold. An excellent accompaniment to cold cuts and salads.

Useful hint
If slivered almonds are not available, blanch and skin some whole almonds. Leave them to dry for a few minutes before carefully cutting them lengthwise into slivers.

Whole Stuffed Sautéed Courgettes
Tori Bhari hui

Although this dish sounds slightly complicated, it is in fact very easy to make. The addition of lemon juice while sautéing the courgettes brings out their best flavour.

Serves 4
Preparation time: 20 minutes
Cooking time: 20 minutes

450g/1 lb baby courgettes (at least 8)
1 medium onion
1 clove of garlic
2 medium tomatoes
2 tablespoons oil
1 teaspoon cumin seeds

50g/2 oz frozen corn
1 tablespoon finely chopped coriander leaves
1 teaspoon salt
1/2 teaspoon chilli powder
50g/2 oz butter or ghee
Juice of 1 lemon

1. Thoroughly wash and dry the courgettes. Cut off the

stalks and a little bit at the other ends. Cut the courgettes into halves lengthwise.

2. With a teaspoon, carefully scoop out all the inside pulp of the courgettes, leaving bare courgette shells. Keeping the pairs together, soak these shells in a little salted cold water.

3. Finely chop the onion and crush the garlic. Scorch the tomatoes over a naked flame and remove their skins. Cut them into halves and deseed, then cut them finely. Cut the courgette pulp up finely.

4. Heat a frying pan or *karahi* then add the oil. When hot, add the cumin seeds and, as soon as they pop, add the onion and garlic.

5. Stir-fry for a few minutes until the onions are a pale golden colour. Add the tomatoes, courgette pulp, corn and coriander leaves. Stir-fry for a few minutes then add the salt and chilli powder.

6. Mix well then cover, reduce the heat and cook for a few minutes until the mixture is soft. Remove and rinse out the pan.

7. Meanwhile, remove the courgette shells from the water. Carefully dry them with a clean kitchen towel or paper.

8. Remove the cooked courgette mixture from the heat and leave to cool for a few minutes. Then carefully pile the mixture generously into one section of each courgette shell. Place the empty halves on top so that the mixture is completely covered.

9. Break off a long length of cotton and wind this around the stuffed courgette to hold the two halves together. This will prevent any stuffing from oozing out while sauté-ing.

10. Heat the butter or ghee in the frying pan that was used to cook the mixture. When the butter is frothing, carefully place the courgettes in the pan and sauté over a medium heat.

11. Stir carefully, making sure that the courgettes are thoroughly cooked on all sides. Add the lemon juice, increase

the heat and cook the courgettes until the lemon juice has evaporated.

12. Have a serving dish warm and ready. Remove the cotton, place the courgettes on the dish and serve at once.

Serving suggestion
These courgettes are excellent as a hot starter to a meal, or as part of the main course.

⊷∘⊶

Stuffed Whole Cauliflower
Saabat Bhari hui Phoolgobi

Cauliflower is one of the blandest of vegetables, so it is a good idea to liven it up with something exciting. In this recipe I have stuffed the space in between the florets with a delicious spicy coconut chutney.

Serves 4
Preparation time: 20 minutes plus 20 minutes boiling
Cooking time: 20 minutes

1 medium-sized cauliflower
$^1/_2$ teaspoon salt

Chutney

100g/4 oz freshly grated coconut
2 green chillies
3 tablespoons freshly chopped coriander leaves
2 tablespoons lemon juice
1 teaspoon sugar
1 teaspoon salt
2 tablespoons (approx.) water
2 tablespoons oil
Rind of 1 lemon, finely grated

1. Remove the tough outer stalks from around the cauliflower. Wash thoroughly in running water.
2. Place the cauliflower upside down in a large pan with the salt and enough water to cover it.
3. Bring to the boil, then reduce the heat and simmer until the florets are tender. Drain carefully, transfer the cauliflower to a shallow ovenproof dish and allow to cool.
4. Prepare the chutney by placing the coconut, green chillies, coriander leaves, lemon juice, sugar and salt in a liquidizer. Grind to a smooth paste.
5. Add a little water if the chutney is too thick.
6. Carefully stuff some of the chutney in the spaces between the florets, keeping a little bit to be spread on the top.
7. Glaze the top of the cauliflower with oil and cook for 15–20 minutes in a preheated oven – gas 4/180°C/350°F – until the top is lightly browned.
8. Serve hot, sprinkled with finely grated lemon rind.

Note: It is important to remove all the white pith from the lemon rind otherwise it will turn bitter. If fresh coconut is not available, use desiccated coconut which has been moistened with some warm water before use.

Serving suggestion
Serve hot with paranthas (page 213).

Cauliflower in Tomato and Spices
Phoolgobi ka Bhartha

In this recipe I have used a mixture of spicy onions, tomatoes and mint to liven up the cauliflower. A hint to boiled-cauliflower lovers: add a couple of pieces of stale bread to the water to absorb the smell of boiling cauliflower, or a small pinch of dried or fresh mint.

Serves 4
Preparation time: 25 minutes
Cooking time: 20 minutes

1 medium-sized cauliflower	2 tablespoons oil
2 medium onions	1–2 green chillies
Small piece of fresh ginger	1 teaspoon salt
1 clove of garlic	$1/4$ teaspoon turmeric
1 teaspoon dried mint or a	100g/4 oz fresh or canned
small sprig of fresh mint	tomatoes

1. Wash and coarsely grate the cauliflower, including the thick centre stem if it is tender and any of the tender green stalks which surround the base of the cauliflower. (Don't throw away the outer stalks as they can be used for another recipe.)
2. Finely chop the onions. Grind together the ginger, garlic, mint and green chillies to a smooth paste.
3. Heat the oil, add the onions and sauté them, stirring frequently, to a rich golden brown. Take care not to overbrown them or the final appearance of the dish will be ruined.
4. Add the ginger and garlic paste and stir it into the onion mixture. Fry for another minute then add the salt, turmeric and tomatoes.
5. Again stirring frequently, fry this mixture until the tomatoes are reduced to a pulp.
6. Add the cauliflower, stir it into the mixture and cover with a tight-fitting lid. Reduce the heat and cook for about 7–10 minutes without stirring.
7. Remove the lid, increase the heat and, stirring continuously, fry the mixture until all the excess moisture has evaporated.

Although it makes an excellent accompaniment to the main course, I have often served this dish as a snack or drinks starter, in which case you need ordinary white or brown bread or french bread cut into very thin squares, triangles or rounds. Either crisply fry this bread in butter or toast it (much healthier), then place a spoonful of the cauliflower mixture on each little piece of bread. Place a thin slice of processed cheese or coarsely grated Cheddar on top and grill under a hot grill until the cheese begins to melt. Serve hot at once. (Don't serve too many of these if an equally delicious dinner is to follow, as they soon become an addiction.)

❧

Baked Spinach and Cheese
Dum Saag Paneer

A classic dish of northern India in which the soft homemade cheese is cut into cubes, deep-fried and added to the spinach. I find that baking the dish at the end of the cooking process gives it a lovely brown glaze and creates a different taste altogether.

Serves 4
Preparation time: 30 minutes
Cooking time: 1 hour

450g/1 lb frozen or 1kg/2 lbs fresh spinach
175g/6 oz paneer (page 44)
1 tablespoon oil
1 teaspoon cumin seeds
1 medium onion, finely chopped

1 clove of garlic, crushed
1 teaspoon ground coriander
$^1/_2$ teaspoon garam masala
1 teaspoon salt
$^1/_2$ teaspoon chilli powder

138

Garnish (Tarka)

1 tablespoon ghee
1 medium onion, finely
  sliced
2.5cm/1-inch piece of fresh
  ginger, finely sliced

1 fresh green chilli, finely
  chopped

1. Thoroughly wash the spinach if fresh, chop it coarsely, place in a saucepan with a little water and cook for a few minutes to tenderize it. Remove from pan and purée it. (If very small tender leaves are used, then do not purée them.) If frozen spinach is used, completely thaw it out.

2. Prepare the paneer and, once it has had most of the water drained, place it in a food processor and switch on for a few seconds in order to break down the cheese lumps. (If you don't own a food processor, place the cheese on a clean surface and soften it by rubbing it on the surface with the palm of your hand.)

3. Heat the oil, add cumin seeds and, as soon as they pop, add the onion and garlic. Stir-fry to a pale golden colour.

4. Add the coriander, garam masala, salt and chilli powder, stir-fry for another few seconds, then add the spinach. Stir well, reduce heat and leave the spinach to cook until it is well blended with the spices and the moisture has evaporated.

5. Lightly grease a flan dish or loose-bottomed sandwich tin. Divide the cheese into two. Press one half firmly on to the base of the dish or tin.

6. Carefully pour the prepared spinach on top.

7. Spread out the other half into a round no thicker than 5mm/¼ inch thick. Cut thin strips and place on top of the spinach in a lattice pattern.

8. Glaze cheese with a little ghee and bake in a preheated oven – gas 5/190°C/375°F – for 15 minutes until the cheese is lightly browned.

9. Carefully release the bottom and transfer the cheese and

spinach bake on to a serving dish or serve in the flan dish.

10. To prepare the *tarka*, heat the ghee in a small frying pan and add the onion and ginger. Stir-fry to a crisp golden brown, add the green chilli and cook for another few seconds.

11. Pour this sizzling *tarka* on top of the spinach cheese cake and serve at once.

Serving suggestion
This delicious dish is best served with a baked channa dal (page 166) and chappatis (page 211) or nan (page 222).

Spicy Black Chickpeas and Spinach
Kale Channe Palak Wale

Nothing can quite match the sweet taste of tender young spinach leaves. This recipe is certainly a family favourite whenever fresh young spinach is available. The spinach is first lightly blanched, then added to the spicy black chickpeas and, to give the dish its final touch, a glassful of sherry is added just before serving.

Serves 4
Preparation time: 30 minutes plus 24 hours soaking
Cooking time: 1¹/₂ hours

225g/8 oz black chickpeas
1 litre/1¾ pints water
450g/1 lb small spinach leaves
2 tablespoons oil
1 teaspoon ajowan seeds
2 medium onions, finely chopped
2.5cm/1-inch piece of fresh ginger, finely chopped
2 cloves of garlic, finely chopped
2 green chillies, finely chopped
1½ teaspoons salt
4 ripe tomatoes, roughly chopped
3 tablespoons sherry
1 teaspoon garam masala

1. Thoroughly wash the peas in a few changes of water, then leave to soak in fresh water for 24 hours.
2. Drain and rinse the peas and place it in a saucepan with the water. Boil until tender (if pressure-cooked, follow the manufacturer's instructions).
3. Strain, reserving the liquid stock.
4. Thoroughly wash the spinach leaves, then blanch in boiling water for 5 minutes. Drain and keep aside.
5. Heat the oil, add the ajowan seeds and, as soon as they splutter, add the onions, ginger and garlic. Stir-fry until the onions are a golden brown.
6. Add the green chillies and salt. Stir-fry for a few seconds. Then add the tomatoes and continue frying over low heat until they become soft (pour in a little of the reserved stock if necessary).
7. Add the boiled peas and blanched spinach. Stir well and add 150ml/¼ pint of the reserved stock. Mix well, partially cover and leave to cook until all the moisture has dried up.
8. Pour in the sherry and sprinkle the garam masala on top. Mix well and serve at once.

Serving suggestion
Serve hot as part of the main meal with plain boiled rice (page 184), natural yogurt (page 47) and tossed salad.

Broccoli in Ajowan and Yogurt
Ajowan Wali Hari Phoolgobi

Broccoli belongs to the same family as the white cauliflower. A common vegetable now that it can be frozen, it was once a luxury. It is a delicate vegetable and should be accorded the same respect as that given to asparagus. The best way to cook broccoli, whether fresh or frozen, is to tie it into small bundles and plunge it into boiling water for the minimum time to make it tender but not soggy. The addition of yogurt and ajowan not only enhances the flavour of broccoli but also helps to counteract the 'wind' problem caused in the stomach.

Serves 4
Preparation time: 10 minutes
Cooking time: 30 minutes

675g/1½ lbs fresh or frozen
  broccoli
1 teaspoon salt
½ teaspoon coarsely ground
  black pepper
2 teaspoons gram flour

200ml/6 fl.oz natural yogurt
1 tablespoon oil
1 teaspoon ajowan seeds
½ teaspoon salt
4 small red chillies

1. Thoroughly wash the fresh broccoli. (There is no need to thaw out frozen broccoli.) Have a large pan of salted boiling water ready. Add the black pepper to it. Boil rapidly for a minute then add the broccoli and cook for about 7–8 minutes so that the broccoli is partly cooked. Drain and transfer to a shallow ovenproof dish. Keep warm.
2. Sieve the gram flour into the yogurt. Lightly whip the yogurt so that the flour lumps are broken up.
3. Heat the oil and add the ajowan seeds, which will pop and splutter at once. Remove the pan from heat, pour in the

yogurt mix, add the salt and chillies, return the pan to the heat and, stirring constantly, bring the yogurt to just boiling point (this will cook the gram flour and prevent the yogurt from curdling).

4. Pour the cooked yogurt over the parboiled broccoli, cover and bake in a preheated oven – gas 6/200°C/400°F – for about 15 minutes.

5. Serve piping hot straight out of the oven, as reheating will ruin the broccoli.

Serving suggestion
Serve as a separate vegetable course or part of the main meal in which no yogurt has been used.

❦

Mixed Vegetables
Milihui Sabji

Mixed vegetables immediately bring to mind a packet of the frozen variety. In this recipe the mixed vegetables are different: aubergines, green and red peppers, courgettes and tomatoes – a sort of ratatouille, but spicier.

Serves 4
Preparation time: 25 minutes
Cooking time: 25 minutes

1 large aubergine, sliced into thick rounds
3 courgettes, thickly sliced
2 tablespoons oil
1 teaspoon cumin seeds
2 medium onions, coarsely sliced
2 cloves of garlic, crushed
2 green peppers, quartered
1 red pepper, quartered
1¼ teaspoons salt
½ teaspoon chilli powder
3 tomatoes, roughly chopped
½ teaspoon garam masala
1 tablespoon chopped coriander leaves

1. Soak the aubergine and courgette slices in cold water to prevent discoloration.
2. Heat oil, add the cumin seeds and, as soon as they pop and splutter, add the onions and garlic. Stir-fry until the onions turn a pale golden colour.
3. Drain the aubergines and courgettes and add them to the onions along with the red and green peppers. Stir-fry for a few minutes then add the salt, chilli powder and tomatoes.
4. Mix well, reduce the heat, cover and allow to cook until the vegetables are tender but still retain their shape.
5. Transfer to a serving dish, sprinkle garam masala and chopped coriander on top and serve.

Serving suggestion
Serve as an accompaniment to a main course such as meat, poultry along with rice or chappatis (page 211).

Roasted Red and Green Peppers
Simla Mirch ka Bhartha

Aubergines are traditionally used for this Punjabi dish, in which the aubergines are roasted over a naked flame, preferably over charcoal, to give it its unique flavour. In this dish I have recreated the *bhartha* using red and green peppers which are roasted under a naked flame so that the skin is completely scorched. This method gives the peppers a unique flavour.

Serves 4
Preparation time: 10 minutes plus 10 minutes roasting
Cooking time: 20 minutes

3 green peppers
3 red peppers
2 tablespoons oil
2 medium onions, finely chopped
1 clove of garlic, crushed
1cm/^{1}/$_2$-inch piece of fresh ginger, finely chopped

^{1}/$_2$ teaspoon chilli powder
^{1}/$_4$ teaspoon turmeric
1 teaspoon salt
2 ripe tomatoes, coarsely chopped

1. Place the 6 peppers on the mesh over a naked flame or under a hot grill. Keep turning them so that the skins are scorched on all sides.
2. Once they are done, remove and carefully peel off all the scorched skin. Remove the stalks and seeds and cut the peppers into small pieces.
3. Heat the oil and add the onions, garlic and ginger. Stir-fry until the onions turn a rich golden colour.
4. Add the chilli powder, turmeric and salt and cook for another few seconds.

145

5. Add the tomatoes and, stirring frequently, fry the mixture until the tomatoes have softened slightly.
6. To this mixture, add the roasted chopped peppers. Stir-fry for a few minutes, then reduce the heat, cover and allow to cook for a further 8–10 minutes, giving the ingredients time to blend with each other.

Serving suggestion
Serve hot as an accompaniment to the main course.

Stuffed Squash with Peppers
Bharve Tinde Mirch Wale

Tinda, or squash melon, is a native of India and very popular in the Punjab. There is a small round variety which is either pale or a darker green with very fine tiny hairs on the skin. However the pale green variety is considered the better of the two and is usually available in most Indian grocery stores. The small vegetable can be stuffed with a variety of ingredients, and in this recipe I have used a spicy mixture of red and green peppers and mango powder.

Serves 4
Preparation time: 25 minutes
Cooking time: 45 minutes

8 medium-sized tinda
1 medium onion
Small piece of ginger
1 clove of garlic
1 green chilli
A few coriander leaves
1 green pepper

1 red pepper
2 tablespoons oil
1 teaspoon cumin seeds
1 teaspoon salt
1½ teaspoons mango powder

1. Lightly scrape off the tinda skin. Cut a slice from each stalk end and retain the slices. Very carefully scoop out the insides which consist of a soft white pulp with tiny seeds. Brush the outsides of the tinda skins with a little oil. Chop up the white pulp.
2. Finely mince the onion, ginger, garlic and the green chilli. Finely chop the coriander leaves.
3. Remove the stalks, white pith and seeds from the two peppers. Chop finely.
4. Heat the oil, add the cumin seeds and, as soon as they pop, add the ground onion mixture. Stirring frequently, fry to a pale golden colour (add a spoonful of water if necessary to prevent it from sticking to the bottom).
5. Add the red and green peppers and the chopped tinda pulp, salt and mango powder. Reduce the heat and sauté for a few minutes to soften the peppers slightly.
6. Remove from the heat and carefully spoon the mixture into the empty tinda shells. Replace the top slices to cover the stuffing.
7. Place in an ovenproof shallow dish and bake in a preheated oven – gas 5/190°C/375°F – for about 35 minutes, until the tinda shells are soft but not broken up.
8. Serve immediately.

Note: If tinda are not available, substitute with marrow or courgettes, in which case halve the marrow or courgettes lengthwise, scoop out the seeds and pulp and proceed as for this recipe.

Serving suggestion
A delicious dish that can double up as a starter or as part of the main meal with rice, yogurt and dal or meat.

Large Stuffed Tomatoes with Spicy Corn
Bharve Tamater Makki Wale

Whenever I see really large, luscious-looking ripe tomatoes my imagination runs riot with the stuffing I might use with them. In this recipe I have chosen frozen corn which is fried with lots of fresh coriander leaves and cumin seeds to enhance the flavour of corn and tomato. If large tomatoes are not available then use large mushrooms and proceed in the same way.

Serves 4
Preparation time: 20 minutes
Cooking time: 30 minutes

4 large or 8 smaller tomatoes
2 medium onions
2 tablespoons chopped
    coriander leaves
Small piece of fresh ginger
1 clove of garlic

2 green chillies
2 tablespoons oil
1 teaspoon cumin seeds
1 teaspoon salt
¼ teaspoon turmeric
175g/6 oz frozen corn

1. Prepare the tomatoes by cutting off a thick slice at the stalk end. Using a teaspoon, carefully scoop out all the pulp and the seeds (reserve them for another dish).
2. Using the tip of a sharp knife, carefully cut the skin all the way round the tomato. (Do not cut through the tomato.)
3. Finely chop the onions and coriander leaves.
4. Grind the ginger, garlic and green chillies to a fine paste.
5. Heat the oil, add cumin seeds and, as soon as they pop, add the chopped onions and, stirring frequently, fry to a pale golden colour.
6. Add the ground ginger paste and mix it into the onions. Cook for another couple of minutes.
7. Sprinkle the salt and turmeric on top along with the frozen

corn (there is no need to thaw it) and the chopped coriander leaves.

8. Reduce the heat, cover and cook for about 15 minutes until the corn is tender, stirring occasionally to ensure that the mixture doesn't stick to the bottom of the pan.

9. Place the prepared tomatoes in a lightly greased ovenproof dish. Stuff the corn mixture into the empty tomato cases so that they are piled up high. Cover with foil or with a lid.

10. Place the ovenproof dish in the preheated oven – gas 4/180°C/350°F – for about 20 minutes, until the tomatoes are slightly soft.

Serving suggestion
Serve as a part of the main course, or as a separate vegetable course with just plain homemade yogurt (page 47) to which salt and black pepper has been added.

❧

Bitter Gourd with Tomatoes
Karele aur Tamater ki Sabji

A bright green vegetable with a knobbly skin and pointed ends, the bitter gourd is now available in most oriental stores. As its name suggests, this vegetable has an extremely bitter taste if not treated first. In order to remove the bitterness, scrape off the skin, slit (if using whole) or cut into thin slices. Remove the seeds if tough, then sprinkle the flesh generously with salt. Rub in the salt, place the gourds in a colander or in a sieve, or on a plate in a pile (tip the plate slightly) and leave them for 4–5 hours. Then thoroughly wash them under a running cold tap to remove all traces of salt and bitter water. Use them as required, either stuffed with onions and spices or sautéed with tomatoes and onions. A slightly acquired taste but absolutely delicious.

Serves 4
Preparation time: 20 minutes plus 4–5 hours draining
Cooking time: 30 minutes

6 large bitter gourds
3 medium onions
225g/8 oz fresh ripe
  tomatoes
2 green chillies

2 teaspoons coriander seeds
2 tablespoons oil
1 teaspoon salt
$\frac{1}{2}$ teaspoon turmeric

1. Prepare and slice the bitter gourds as described. After washing thoroughly, leave to drain for a few minutes.
2. Finely chop the onions, tomatoes and green chillies.
3. Lightly crush the coriander seeds.
4. Heat the oil, add the coriander seeds and fry for a second then add the onions.
5. Stirring frequently, fry the onions to a rich golden colour.
6. Add the tomatoes, green chillies, salt and turmeric. Stirring frequently, fry the mixture until the tomatoes are reduced to a pulp and most of the excess water has dried up.
7. Add the prepared bitter gourds and stir them into the onion and tomato mixture. Cover, reduce the heat to low and, stirring occasionally, cook until the gourds are tender but still have a bite to them.

Serving suggestion
Serve as part of the main meal with either rice or chappatis (page 211) and a dal and yogurt.

Spicy Swede with Tomatoes
Swede ka Bhartha

One vegetable that I have never seen in India is swede, a subtly perfumed fibrous vegetable that also has a very delicate yellow-pinkish colour. When I first came to England I was very hesitant to try this large round vegetable: I thought that as it resembled a small yam it probably tasted like one. Imagine my surprise when I finally tasted it. It is now a firm favourite when cooked with spices.

Serves 4
Preparation time: 25 minutes
Cooking time: 40 minutes

675g/1½ lbs swedes	1 teaspoon cumin seeds
Water to boil	½ teaspoon chilli powder
2 medium onions	¼ teaspoon turmeric
1 clove of garlic	1¼ teaspoons salt
2.5cm/1-inch piece of fresh ginger	1 tablespoon chopped coriander leaves
225g/8 oz ripe tomatoes	1 teaspoon garam masala
2 tablespoons oil	

1. Wash and peel the swedes. Cut them into small chunks and place in a saucepan with enough water to cover. Bring to the boil and continue cooking until the swedes are tender.
2. Drain (reserve the liquid for soup or to cook a dal in). Completely mash the swedes with a potato masher.
3. While the swedes are boiling, prepare the rest of the ingredients. Finely slice the onions, crush the garlic and slice the ginger.
4. Wash the tomatoes and cut them into small pieces.
5. Heat the oil, add the cumin seeds and, as soon as they pop,

151

add the onions, ginger and garlic. Stirring frequently, fry this mixture to a rich golden brown. (Care must be taken not to overbrown the onions as they will spoil the appearance of the dish.)

6. Add the chilli powder, turmeric and salt, mix in these ingredients and cook for another minute or so. Then add the chopped tomatoes and coriander.

7. Stir-fry the mixture until the tomatoes are reduced to a pulp and are well blended.

8. Stir in the mashed swede and, stirring frequently, cook for another 10 minutes or so until the swede is well blended with the rest of the ingredients.

9. Sprinkle the garam masala on top and serve.

Serving suggestion
Serve as part of the main meal where a meat or poultry dish is also included.

⊷⊶

Soft Cheese and Nigella Seed Mixture
Paneer aur Kalonji ke Sabji

Protein, be it from lentils, meat or from dairy products, is essential for the wellbeing of our bodies. The cheese is gently cooked in a spicy tomato and onion mixture, for only afew minutes as prolonged cooking tends to toughen the cheese.

Serves 4–6
Preparation time: 20 minutes plus 30 minutes draining
Cooking time: 20 minutes

175g/6 oz paneer (page 44)
2 medium onions
1 clove of garlic
100g/4 oz ripe fresh or
  canned tomatoes
1 tablespoon chopped
  coriander leaves

2 tablespoons oil
1 teaspoon nigella seeds
1/4 teaspoon turmeric
1/2 teaspoon chilli powder
1 teaspoon salt

1. As soon as the paneer has been strained, rinse it under a cold tap and keep crumbling it until no large lumps remain.
2. Tie up the ends of the cloth and hang it up to drain for about 30 minutes. Remove from the cheese cloth and once again crumble it between your fingers.
3. Finely chop the onions, garlic, tomatoes and coriander leaves.
4. Heat the oil, add the nigella seeds and, within a few seconds, add the onion and garlic.
5. Stirring frequently, fry the mixture to a rich golden colour, taking care not to overbrown the onions.
6. Add the turmeric, chilli powder and salt. Fry for another few seconds then add the tomatoes. Continue stirring and cook the mixture until the tomatoes are reduced to a pulp.
7. Add the crumbled cheese, mix it in well and, stirring gently, cook the mixture for another few minutes. (As the cheese is already cooked it only has to be warmed through.)
8. Sprinkle the chopped coriander on top, mix it in with the cheese and tomatoes and serve hot.

Serving suggestion
Serve as part of the main meal.

Turnips Cooked in Aniseed
Shalgam Saunf ke Saath

Aniseed, a delicate spice yet full of flavour, is very rarely included in savoury dishes. In India it is generally used in the Kashmiri style of cooking, or as a seed that is brewed in tea to cure colds and coughs, or eaten as an after-dinner spice to aid digestion. The delicate flavours of turnip and aniseed blend well together in this particular dish.

Serves 4
Preparation time: 20 minutes
Cooking time: 25 minutes

450g/1 lb small young
  turnips
2 medium onions
2 ripe tomatoes
1 teaspoon aniseeds
2 tablespoons oil
$^1/_2$ teaspoon nigella seeds

$^1/_4$ teaspoon turmeric
$^1/_4$ teaspoon chilli powder
1 teaspoon salt
100g/4 oz frozen or fresh
  shelled peas
Small bunch of fresh dill,
  coarsely chopped

1. Peel and cut the turnips into small pieces.
2. Finely slice the onions and chop the tomatoes. Lightly crush the aniseeds.
3. Heat the oil, add the aniseeds and nigella seeds, and within a few seconds add the onion. Stirring frequently, fry the onion to a pale golden colour.
4. Add the turmeric, chilli powder and salt, mix well, then add the tomatoes. Reduce the heat and, stirring frequently, allow the tomatoes to become soft and pulpy.
5. Add the peas and the turnips. Mix well and reduce the heat to low, cover with a tight-fitting lid and cook for about

20 minutes until the turnips become tender and all the excess moisture dries up.

6. Transfer on to a serving dish and sprinkle some dill on top.

Serving suggestion
Turnips go well with lamb, along with a crunchy okra in yogurt (page 204) and either parantha (page 213) or plain rice.

⬥⬥⬥

Kubba's Sweet and Sour Aubergines
Kubba's Khate Meethe Baingan

This unusual combination of aubergines and puréed green peas makes a very colourful and, indeed, a unique dish. The saffron imparts its delicate flavour through the water in which the aubergine is baked. A highly recommended dish.

Serves 6
Preparation time: 35 minutes plus 1 hour salting
Cooking time: 45 minutes

275g/10 oz frozen green peas
1 teaspoon garam masala
1 teaspoon baking powder
1 teaspoon salt
1/2 teaspoon freshly ground
  black pepper
3 medium-sized plump
  aubergines

Oil for deep-frying
150ml/1/4 pint water
150ml/1/4 pint wine vinegar
50g/2 oz sugar
Small pinch of saffron (8–10
  strands)

1. Gently simmer the peas in a little water until tender.
2. Drain and purée the peas in a food processor, blender or through a sieve.

3. Add the garam masala, baking powder, salt and black pepper. Whip to a smooth consistency. Cover and set aside.
4. Wash and dry the aubergines. Cut in half lengthwise, right through the stalk.
5. Using the tip of a sharp knife, make an incision around the aubergine leaving a rim of about 1cm/^{1}/$_2$ inch thickness.
6. Carefully scoop out all the flesh, making sure that the skin shell is not damaged. (Sprinkle the scooped-out flesh with salt to avoid discolouration and use for another recipe.)
7. Sprinkle the shells with some salt and set aside for about 1 hour. (This will remove any excess moisture.)
8. Thoroughly wash and dry the shells.
9. Heat the oil and deep-fry the shells for a few minutes in order to soften them slightly. Drain and place in a shallow ovenproof dish.
10. Carefully fill the fried shells with the pea purée.
11. Mix together the water, vinegar, sugar and saffron. Stir to dissolve the sugar.
12. Pour this sweetened mixture into the shallow ovenproof dish. (None of the liquid should be poured into the filled aubergines.)
13. Bake in a preheated oven – gas 5/190°C/375°F – for about 30 minutes.
14. Remove from the oven and serve at once.

Serving suggestion
Serve as a vegetable course without any accompaniment other than crisply fried chappatis.

Spicy Sour Aubergines
Masaledar Khate Baingan

Aubergines come in all shapes, sizes and, indeed, colours. The shapes vary from long and thin to round and fat, and their colours range from white to dark purple. But on my last trip to India, I saw for the first time some beautiful thin long green aubergines. If you cannot find green aubergines, use purple ones instead.

Serves 4
Preparation time: 20 minutes
Cooking time: 30 minutes

8 small round aubergines
6 tablespoons oil for frying
2 tablespoons ground
  coriander
1 tablespoon ground cumin
2 tablespoons mango
  powder

1 teaspoon garam masala
1/2 teaspoon chilli powder
1 teaspoon salt
1 teaspoon tomato purée
3 tablespoons water
3 tablespoons freshly
  chopped coriander leaves

1. Wash and thoroughly dry the aubergines. Carefully slice each one into four, leaving the slices attached at the stalk.
2. Heat the oil in a frying pan or *karahi*. Fry 2–3 aubergines at a time for a few minutes, turning over once, to soften the skins. Drain and place on kitchen paper. Fry the remaining aubergines.
3. While the aubergines are cooling, prepare the stuffing. Mix together the spices and salt with the tomato purée and water to a thick paste.
4. Carefully lift up the aubergine segments and stuff some of the paste into them. Repeat until all the aubergines and the paste have been used up.

5. Place the aubergines in a baking dish, cover with a lid or foil and bake in a warm oven – gas 4/180°C/350°F – for 20 minutes until the stuffing has really soaked into the aubergines.
6. Remove the lid, sprinkle the coriander on top and serve.

Serving suggestion
I find these aubergines served cold make an excellent starter to the meal, but serve them hot if they are part of the main meal.

❧

Mushrooms Stuffed with Soft Cheese
Bharvi Khumba aur Paneer

Cultivated mushrooms such as we know in the West have recently become available and popular in the larger cities of India. Choose the mushrooms that are white, free from any discolouring and firm to the touch. For this recipe you need the larger mushrooms, to hold the stuffing.

Serves 4
Preparation time: 20 minutes
Cooking time: 30 minutes

10–12 large mushrooms
50g/2 oz homemade paneer (page 44)
2 ripe tomatoes
2 tablespoons oil
1 teaspoon cumin seeds

$\frac{1}{2}$ teaspoon chilli powder
$\frac{1}{4}$ teaspoon turmeric
1 teaspoon salt
$\frac{1}{2}$ teaspoon garam masala
1 tablespoon chopped coriander leaves

1. Gently wash the mushrooms. Wipe dry and remove the stalks (use them in soups or other sauces).

158

2. Finely crumble the cheese. Skin the tomatoes and remove the seeds. Chop them finely.
3. Heat the oil and sauté the mushrooms in it for just a minute, remove and drain on absorbent paper.
4. Into the same oil add the cumin seeds, and as soon as they pop add the chilli powder, turmeric, salt and tomatoes. Stir-fry for a minute or so.
5. Add the crumbled paneer, garam masala and coriander.
6. Stirring continuously, fry the mixture for another 5 minutes so that all the ingredients are well blended.
7. Spoon the mixture into the mushrooms and place them in a lightly greased shallow ovenproof dish. Cover with foil or a lid.
8. Place the dish in a preheated oven – gas 5/190°C/375°F – for about 30 minutes.

Serving suggestion
Serve as a starter or as part of the main meal.

❂

Stuffed Spinach Eggs
Bharve Ande Palak Wale

The three delightful colours of this dish – white, green and yellow – make it a most appetizing combination. I have stuffed hardboiled eggs with a spicy spinach mixture which is sprinkled with the yellow yolks. To give this dish some crunchiness, add some crispy fried onions and ginger. A delight to the eye and to the palate.

Serves 4
Preparation time: 20 minutes
Cooking time: 30 minutes

6 large eggs
225g/8 oz frozen spinach or
   450g/1 lb fresh spinach
1 clove of garlic
1 green chilli
6–8 whole black peppercorns
2 tablespoons oil
1 teaspoon cumin seeds

Pinch of asafoetida
1 teaspoon salt
1 tablespoon ghee
1 small onion, peeled and
   finely sliced
2.5cm/1-inch piece of fresh
   ginger, peeled and finely
   sliced

1. Hardboil the eggs the way you like them. Peel and cut in half lengthwise.
2. If frozen spinach is being used, thaw it out. If using fresh spinach, carefully wash and shake dry the leaves (use only the small tender leaves). Chop finely.
3. Finely grind the garlic and green chilli. Coarsely grind the black pepper.
4. Heat the oil, add the cumin seeds and, as soon as they pop, add the asafoetida. Then at once add the garlic and green chilli. Stir-fry for a few seconds then add the spinach, salt and black pepper.
5. Stir the mixture, cover and cook over a low heat until the excess moisture dries up. (If fresh spinach has been used, purée it in the food processor or blender to a smooth consistency.)
6. Scoop out the hardboiled yolks and mash them through a sieve. Add all but the yolk of one egg to the spinach and stir it in really well. This will help to thicken the spinach.
7. Spoon the spinach mixture into the empty egg whites and arrange them on a serving dish.
8. Heat the ghee in a small frying pan, add the onion and ginger, and stir-fry to a crisp golden brown.
9. Carefully sprinkle some of the onion and ginger mixture on top of each egg and pour over a little of the ghee to add extra flavour.
10. Sprinkle some of the finely sieved yolk on top and serve.

Serving suggestion

A delicious, spicy egg dish which will enhance any meal, whether as an accompaniment to the main course or served separately as a starter. If served as a starter, place the eggs on crisp light-green lettuce leaves to enhance the dark green of the spinach.

Freezing hint

Although there is no point in freezing the eggs, it is worth freezing the spinach at the stage before adding the egg yolks. When needed, thaw the spinach, hardboil the eggs and proceed with the rest of the recipe.

⬥⇒◦⇐⬥

Spiced Eggs

Eggs are not used in Indian cooking as a thickening agent, therefore, apart from hardboiling them and cooking them in sauces, there are very few egg dishes in the traditional repertoire. In this recipe I have prepared an onion, tomato and spice mixture, then simply broken the eggs on top and allowed them to set. A version of fried eggs but with a difference.

Serves 4
Preparation time: 20 minutes
Cooking time: 20 minutes

3 medium onions
1 clove of garlic
Small bunch of coriander
   leaves
3 medium tomatoes
2 tablespoons oil
1/2 teaspoon garam masala

1 teaspoon lightly crushed
   aniseeds
1 teaspoon salt
Freshly ground black pepper
   to taste
25g/1 oz blanched slivered
   almonds
4 eggs

1. Coarsely chop the onions, crush the garlic and finely chop the coriander leaves.
2. Roast each tomato by inserting a fork into the stalk end and holding the tomato over a naked flame. The skin will scorch and split open, and the delicious fragrance gives the dish a unique flavour. Remove from the flame and chop the tomatoes finely, with the skins.
3. Heat the oil in a frying pan, add the chopped onions and stir-fry until a pale golden brown and transparent. Add the garlic and tomatoes, continue stir-frying until the mixture is well blended, then add half the chopped coriander leaves, the garam masala, aniseeds, salt and black pepper. Stir-fry for another few minutes to blend all the spices. Finally, add the almond slivers. Stir once again and then cover and cook for 5 minutes in order to infuse the spices. Remove the lid and level the mixture in the pan with the back of a wooden spoon or spatula.
4. Break the eggs straight on to the tomato mixture one at a time, placing them side by side. Cover the pan with the lid and let the eggs cook and set for about 5–7 minutes. Serve hot at once, sprinkled with the remaining coriander leaves.

Serving suggestion
This makes an excellent hot starter to the meal, served with wedges of lemon, or it can be part of the main meal instead of a vegetable dish.

Useful hint
The *masala*, i.e. the onion and tomato mixture, can be made well in advance and then reheated just before serving, the eggs being added at the last minute.

Fresh Coriander Omelette
Dhania ka Omelette

An omelette made with fresh coriander leaves and green chillies is as unique and delicious as the renowned *omelette fines herbes*. I make a base with boiled, sliced and spiced potatoes, then pour the egg mixture on top and either bake it in the oven or cook on top of the stove. Cut into wedges or squares, it can be served at all sorts of occasions.

Serves 4–6
Preparation time: 30 minutes
Cooking time: 25 minutes

225g/8 oz small potatoes
1 medium onion
Small bunch of coriander
  leaves
2 green chillies
4 large eggs
3 tablespoons water

1 teaspoon salt
3 tablespoons ghee
1 teaspoon cumin seeds
1/4 teaspoon freshly ground
  black pepper
1/4 teaspoon garam masala

1. Boil the potatoes in their skins. Peel and slice them into fairly thick slices.
2. Finely chop the onion, coriander leaves and green chillies.
3. Break the eggs into a bowl, add the water, coriander leaves, green chillies and half the salt. Thoroughly beat with a fork without producing too much froth.
4. Heat half the ghee, add the cumin seeds, and as soon as they pop add the sliced potatoes and sauté carefully without breaking them.
5. Sprinkle on the rest of the salt, black pepper and garam masala and continue sautéing, turning the potatoes over until the edges start to become crisp.

163

6. If the omelette is to be baked, transfer the sauté spiced potatoes on to a flan dish. Make sure they cover the entire surface. Pour the beaten egg mixture on top, add the remaining ghee and at once place in a preheated oven – gas 6/200°C/400°F – for about 15–20 minutes until the egg has set.
7. If the omelette is to be cooked on top of the stove, spread out the sauté spiced potatoes in the sauté pan, add a little more of the ghee, pour in the beaten egg mixture. Increase the heat and allow the egg to set. Pour the rest of the ghee around the edges of the omelette and cook until the egg is set.
8. If a grill is available, place the pan under a hot grill for about 4–5 minutes to firm up the top.
9. Remove from the pan, cut into wedges or squares and serve.

Serving suggestion
Excellent starter with drinks or as part of the main meal where no other vegetable dish is served. It would go well with crisp paranthas (page 213), especially as a treat for Sunday morning brunch with ginger lassi (page 256) to drink.

Pulses

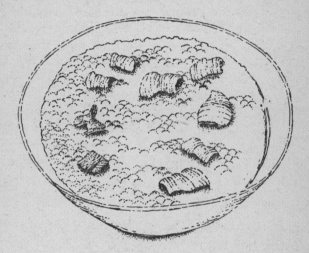

'Beans and pulses remain the same no matter what you do to them,' has been the complaint of my friends. 'They all taste bland and uninteresting.' Because of this bland taste they lend themselves beautifully to all sorts of combinations that enhance their taste and textures.

Whole beans are generally cooked to a mushy consistency. But in this chapter I have boiled them until just tender but still retaining their shape, then tossed them in a combination of spices or topped them with crunchy garnishes, such as roasted coconut or chopped almonds. New tastes have been created by cooking dals (pulses) with fresh mint or giving a sizzling *tarka* (garnish) of dried fenugreek leaves. Baked dals, i.e. dals cooked slowly in the oven like the baked channa dal, create a unique taste all their own. This soft, well-cooked dal I have garnished with a crispy bacon *tarka*. Ajowan is a spice that is not commonly used in dals, yet the ajowan and yogurt *tarka* is just out of this world. I have elected to serve these dals not only with the main meal as an accompaniment but also as a separate course with either rice or chappati, parantha or nan. For the humble dal is both nutritionally valuable and has an intriguing taste which all too often gets lost when served with other highly spiced food.

<hr />

Baked Channa Dal
Oven me Paki Channe ki Dal

Although this dish can be cooked on top of the stove, when slowly baked in the oven the taste is quite delicious.

Serves 4
Preparation time: 10 minutes plus 2 hours soaking
Cooking time: 1¹/₂ hours

225g/8 oz channa dal
750ml/1¹/₄ pints (approx.)
  water

1 teaspoon salt
¹/₄ teaspoon turmeric
Pinch of asafoetida

Garnish (Tarka)
1 tablespoon ghee
1 small onion, finely sliced
1 teaspoon chopped ginger

¹/₂ teaspoon chilli powder
1 teaspoon chopped
  coriander leaves

1. Thoroughly clean and wash the dal until the water runs clear. Leave the dal to soak for at least 2 hours (if the dal is soaked overnight, the result is even better).
2. Rinse the dal once again in clean water. Add the water to

it and place it in the casserole. Add the salt, turmeric and asafoetida. Give the mixture a good stir.

3. Cover with a lid and place in a warm oven – gas 3/170°C/325°F – and leave it to cook for 1½ hours until all the moisture has dried up and the dal is tender and retains its shape.

4. Just before serving, prepare the *tarka* by heating the ghee. When hot, add the onion and ginger.

5. Stir-fry for a few minutes until the onion turns a deep golden brown and crisp. Add the chilli powder. Give the mixture a stir and then immediately pour this over the cooked dal.

6. Sprinkle some freshly chopped coriander leaves on top and serve at once.

Serving suggestion
An excellent accompaniment to a meat or poultry dish. At a formal dinner I often serve this dal as a separate course with just one chappati (page 211). As the taste of the baked dal is unique, it deserves a place of its own.

✐•⊂✐

Channa Dal with Bacon Garnish
Channe ki Dal aur Bacon ka Tarka

In this recipe I have used a crispy bacon *tarka* to enhance an otherwise delicious but bland dal. You can either bake this dal as in the previous recipe or cook it on top of the stove in the more traditional way. It is the unusual garnish that is going to make this a dal of distinction.

Serves 4
Preparation time: 20 minutes plus 1 hour soaking
Cooking time: 40 minutes

125g/5 oz channa dal
750ml/1¼ pints water
1 teaspoon salt

¼ teaspoon turmeric
Small pinch of asafoetida

Garnish (Tarka)
50g/2 oz streaky bacon
1 green chilli

1. Thoroughly wash the dal in a few changes of water until it runs clear. Soak in plenty of cold water for at least 1 hour.
2. Place the dal, water, salt, turmeric and the asafoetida in a medium-sized saucepan. Bring it to the boil, then remove any scum that may form at the top. Reduce the heat, cover and cook for about 35 minutes until the dal is tender and nearly all the moisture has evaporated.
3. Although the consistency of the dal will be moist, the dal itself should retain its shape.
4. Carefully transfer the dal into a serving bowl and keep covered while preparing the *tarka*.
5. Remove the rind and any small bone in the bacon. Cut into small 1cm/½-inch pieces. Remove the chilli stalk and cut the chilli into very thin slices.
6. Heat up a small frying pan, add the bacon and, stirring frequently, fry to a crisp golden brown. Add the sliced chillies towards the end of cooking.
7. Sprinkle this *tarka* over the cooked channa dal and serve at once.

Serving suggestion
This dal can be served as an accompaniment to the main meal, but as I prefer to serve dal as a separate course, I would serve this with two small chappatis (page 211) or one crisp shallow-fried parantha (page 213).

Spicy Moath Beans
Moath ki Chaat

As many varieties of pulses and beans are eaten in India, each region has its own preparations. Although the moath bean takes a fair amount of time to tenderize, unless cooked in a pressure cooker, it is one of my favourites. Its slightly nutty flavour is enhanced by adding just a few spices.

Serves 4
Preparation time: 15 minutes
Cooking time: 1 hour

100g/4 oz moath beans
600ml/1 pint water
1 tablespoon oil
1 medium onion, finely
  sliced
2.5cm/1 inch fresh green
  ginger, finely sliced
1 green chilli, finely chopped

½ teaspoon chilli powder
1 teaspoon salt
½ teaspoon roasted ground
  cumin
2 tablespoons lemon juice
1 tablespoon finely chopped
  coriander leaves

1. Thoroughly clean and wash the moath beans, then place them in a saucepan with the water. Bring to the boil, then reduce the heat and boil gently until they become tender but still hold their shape. (If using a pressure cooker, follow the manufacturer's instructions.)
2. Strain, reserving the liquid for soup. Allow the moath beans to cool (because if fried straight away they will become mushy).
3. Heat the oil, add the cold moath beans and just toss in the hot oil for a few minutes. Transfer on to a serving dish and add all the other ingredients.
4. Mix well and serve.

Serve hot or cold, either as part of the main meal or as a side salad.

❖

Red Kidney Beans with Raw Mango
Rajma Ambi ke Saath

Like all dried beans, red kidney beans must be soaked for at least 12 hours to help them soften. But it is also *essential* to boil red kidney beans for 2–3 hours in a saucepan, or for 20–30 minutes in a pressure cooker. Red kidney beans gently tossed in spices and unripe green mango make an ideal combination.

Serves 4
Preparation time: 20 minutes plus overnight soaking
Cooking time: 3 hours or 30 minutes in a pressure cooker

175g/6 oz red kidney beans
1 litre/1³/₄ pints water
1 teaspoon salt
Small pinch of asafoetida
2 medium onions
1 clove of garlic
2.5cm/1-inch piece of fresh ginger
2 green chillies

1 medium-sized unripe mango
2 tablespoons oil
1 teaspoon cumin seeds
2 tablespoons fresh chopped coriander leaves
¹/₂ teaspoon chilli powder
1 teaspoon garam masala

1. Wash and soak the red kidney beans in plenty of cold water for at least 12 hours.
2. Drain the beans and place them in a saucepan with the water, salt and asafoetida. Bring to the boil, then reduce the heat and allow to boil gently for 2¹/₂–3 hours or until the beans are tender but still hold their shape. Add more

170

water if necessary. (If the beans are to be cooked in a pressure cooker then cook for at least 30 minutes under high pressure and follow the manufacturer's instructions.)

3. Strain off any remaining liquid (and reserve for a soup).
4. Roughly chop the onions, crush the garlic and finely slice the ginger and green chillies. Peel and either coarsely grate or finely slice the mango.
5. Heat the oil, add the cumin seeds and, as soon as they pop, add all the chopped and sliced ingredients.
6. Stir-fry for a minute then add the drained red kidney beans, chilli powder and garam masala.
7. Increase the heat and, stirring continuously, fry this mixture for about 5–10 minutes in order to dry off any moisture.
8. Transfer to a serving dish.

Serving suggestion
Serve hot as part of the main course with meat or poultry and bread, or as a cold/hot salad on its own as a starter.

❖

Moong Bean with Yogurt Tarka
Dahi Wali Moong Saabat

As more and more people are becoming health- and nutrition-conscious, the popularity of the humble moong bean has increased enormously. Sprouted moong beans are no longer restricted to Chinese cooking but are very useful in salads of all cuisines. They are available in most stores, although they are also easy to sprout at home. In this recipe I have used not the sprouted moong beans but the whole bean, and the *tarka* is made with fresh natural yogurt.

Serves 4
Preparation time: 10 minutes
Cooking time: 1 hour

125g/5 oz whole green moong beans
750ml/1¼ pints boiling water

Small pinch of asafoetida
1 teaspoon salt
¼ teaspoon turmeric

Garnish (Tarka)
2 tablespoons natural yogurt
1 tablespoons ghee
1 teaspoon cumin seeds

½ teaspoon chilli powder
1 tablespoon finely chopped coriander leaves

1. Thoroughly clean and wash the moong beans.
2. Place the beans, boiling water, asafoetida, salt and turmeric in the earthenware bowl.
3. Stir to mix all the ingredients. Cover and place in the oven at gas 4/180°C/350°F for about 1 hour.
4. At the end of cooking time the water should have been absorbed and the beans should be tender – split but holding their shape.
5. Carefully remove the bowl from the oven and prepare the *tarka*.
6. Lightly whip the yogurt to a smooth consistency.
7. Heat the ghee, add the cumin seeds and, as soon as they pop, add the chilli powder. At once remove the pan from the heat.
8. Stand well back and add the lightly whipped yogurt to the pan. (It may splutter slightly.)
9. Place the pan back on the fire and, stirring continuously, cook the yogurt for a minute to heat it through.
10. Add the coriander leaves, stir well and pour this over the prepared moong beans and serve.

Serve this delicious dish as an accompaniment to a main course
or as a separate course with crisply fried hot pooris (page
224).

❦

Split Moong Dal with Sesame Seeds
Til aur Moong Dal ka Milan

In this recipe I have used the split moong dal with skins on.
The subtle green-yellow colour is further enhanced by adding
crisply toasted sesame seeds. This dal, like the others, can be
cooked on top of the stove, in the pressure cooker or in the
oven. As the sesame seeds are oily themselves I have preferred
to dry-roast them, but have added a tablespoon of ghee to the
dal during cooking and, instead of pieces of ginger and garlic,
have added just their juice to give the dal more subtle
flavour.

Serves 4–6
Preparation time: 20 minutes plus 30 minutes soaking
Cooking time: 1 hour (or less in a pressure cooker)

175g/6 oz split moong dal
  with skins
900ml/1¹/₂ pints water
Pinch of asafoetida
¹/₄ teaspoon turmeric
1¹/₄ teaspoons salt

2.5cm/1-inch piece of fresh
  ginger
1 clove of garlic
1 green chilli
1 tablespoon ghee

Garnish (Tarka)
2 tablespoons sesame seeds

1. Thoroughly clean and wash the dal and soak it in plenty
   of cold water for at least 30 minutes.

173

2. Drain the dal and put it in a saucepan with the water, asafoetida, turmeric and salt and quickly bring to the boil, then reduce the heat, cover and allow to cook gently, stirring from time to time.
3. Scrape off the ginger skin, grate the ginger and press out its juice. Crush the garlic and press out its juice. Finely grind the green chilli.
4. Halfway through cooking, add the ginger and garlic juices, the chilli and the ghee.
5. Stir the mixture and continue cooking until the dal is tender.
6. Meanwhile, dry-roast the sesame seeds, either under a hot grill or in a frying pan, to a light golden colour. Allow to cool slightly.
7. Pour the dal into a serving dish, sprinkle the roasted sesame seeds on top and serve hot.

Serving suggestion
As with other dals, serve it piping hot either as a separate course with chappati (page 211), or as part of the main course.

Moong Dal with Soft Cheese
Moong Dal Paneer Wali

For this dish I have used the skinless split moong bean. Its kernel is a lovely buttercup yellow in colour and, because its tough skin has been removed, it takes only about 30 minutes to cook in an ordinary pan and even less time in a pressure cooker. Of course you can also bake it in the oven.

Serves 4
Preparation time: 10 minutes plus 30 minutes soaking
Cooking time: 30 minutes (or less in a pressure cooker)

174

175g/6 oz split moong dal (without skins)
600ml/1 pint water
Pinch of asafoetida

1 teaspoon salt
$^1/_4$ teaspoon turmeric
2–3 coriander leaves

Garnish (Tarka)
1 tablespoon ghee
$^1/_2$ teaspoon cumin seeds
50g/2 oz paneer, finely crumbled

$^1/_4$ teaspoon chilli powder

1. Thoroughly clean and wash the dal then soak in cold water for about 30 minutes.
2. Drain the dal and place in a saucepan with the water, asafoetida, salt, turmeric and coriander leaves.
3. Bring to the boil, then reduce the heat to medium, cover and allow to cook until the water has been absorbed and the consistency of the dal is creamy. (If a drier consistency is required, use 150ml/$^1/_4$ pint less water.)
4. Heat the ghee, add the cumin seeds and, as soon as they pop and splutter, add the paneer and, stirring continuously, fry the mixture to a golden colour.
5. Add the chilli powder and continue frying for another minute.
6. Transfer the dal to a serving dish, sprinkle the crisp paneer on top and serve.

Note: The same dal can be baked in the oven. In which case use 300ml/$^1/_2$ pint water and bake it at gas 4/180°C/350°F for about 40–45 minutes. Stir the dal carefully once or twice during cooking. Then proceed with the *tarka* just before serving.

Serving suggestion
Serve hot as part of the main meal, or as a separate course with crisp paranthas (page 213).

Split Moong Dal with Mint
Podine ki Moong Dal

Fresh mint grows in many British gardens, but for those who don't have gardens or who do not grow the herb, I have used dried mint in this recipe.

Serves 4
Preparation time: 10 minutes plus 30 minutes soaking
Cooking time: 35 minutes

175g/6 oz moong dal (split without skins)
Very small piece of fresh ginger
1 tablespoon oil
½ teaspoon cumin seeds
½ teaspoon chilli powder
¼ teaspoon turmeric
½ teaspoon dried mint (or 10 fresh leaves)
1 teaspoon salt
450ml/¾ pint water

1. Thoroughly clean the dal and soak it in plenty of cold water for about 30 minutes.
2. Drain and keep aside.
3. Finely chop the ginger (and the fresh mint leaves if used).
4. Heat the oil and add the cumin seeds and, as soon as they pop, add the chilli powder, turmeric, ginger and mint leaves.
5. Toss the mixture around for a few seconds, then add the drained dal and the salt. Stir well for another minute.
6. Pour in the water, mix well, then reduce the heat, cover and allow to cook gently until the dal is tender and dry – all the moisture should have been absorbed by the dal and its consistency should be fluffy.

Serving suggestion

A different dal with a refreshing taste. Serve it as part of the main meal with a crispy shallow-fried parantha (page 213), lemon and onion salad (page 68) and chicken *raita* (page 201). This would make a lovely light lunch or dinner.

❧

Whole Egyptian Lentils with Fried Coconut
Nariyal Masoor ka Milan

There are two reasons for a *tarka*-garnish: one is to introduce a different flavour and aroma to the otherwise bland dal; the other is to introduce a crunchy texture to contrast with the dal's mushiness. Golden-fried desiccated coconut enhances the flavour and texture of the Egyptian lentils. Split lentils, pink in colour, can be made in the same way, but use less water.

Serves 4
Preparation time: 10 minutes
Cooking time: 1 hour (less in a pressure cooker)

175g/6 oz whole Egyptian lentils	1 litre/1³/₄ pints water
Small piece of fresh ginger	1 teaspoon salt
1 clove of garlic	Small pinch of asafoetida

Garnish (Tarka)
1 green chilli
1 tablespoon ghee
25g/1 oz desiccated coconut

1. Clean and wash the dal in a few changes of water.
2. Peel and finely chop the ginger and crush the garlic.
3. Place the dal, water, salt, asafoetida, garlic and ginger in

a saucepan. Bring it to the boil, then reduce the heat and allow to simmer gently until the dal is tender and almost dry. (Add a little more water if required.) The dal should retain its shape.

4. Carefully transfer the dal to a serving dish.
5. Finely chop the green chilli (if a milder taste is required, slit the chilli, remove its seeds and wash it).
6. Heat the ghee, add the desiccated coconut and green chilli, and, stirring continuously, fry the coconut to a pale golden colour. (Care must be taken not to overbrown the coconut because that will ruin the delicate flavour.)
7. Sprinkle this golden coconut over the dal and serve.

Serving suggestion
As the consistency of the dal is fairly dry, it is best served with some form of bread plus yogurt and either a meat or a poultry dish. I personally prefer to serve dals on their own as a separate course with bread or rice.

❧⊃◦⊂❧

Whole Urad with Dried Fenugreek Leaves
Ma Saabat Sookhi Methi Wali

The whole black bean is unique to the cooking of northern India, whereas the split skinless black bean and its flour are a speciality of the south. Traditionally this bean is cooked over low heat for several hours until it reaches a creamy consistency, but in this recipe I have intentionally cooked the bean just enough for it to be tender but still retain its shape. As the bean takes a long time to become tender, you can use a pressure cooker to speed up the process. A totally different flavour is created by the dried fenugreek leaves added to the dal at the last minute.

Serves 4–6
Preparation time: 10 minutes
Cooking time: 3 hours

125g/5 oz whole black urad
1¼ litres/2 pints water
Small pinch of asafoetida
1¼ teaspoons salt
Small piece of fresh ginger,
  finely chopped

1 clove of garlic, finely
  chopped
1 green chilli, finely chopped

Garnish (Tarka)
2 tablespoons dried
  fenugreek leaves

2 tablespoons ghee

1. Thoroughly clean and wash the urad in a few changes of water.
2. Place it in a saucepan along with the water, asafoetida, salt, ginger, garlic and green chilli.
3. Bring it to the boil, then reduce the heat to medium, cover and allow to simmer until the bean has split, is tender but still holds its shape and is slightly moist. (By that I mean that most of the water should have evaporated.)
4. Transfer on to a serving dish. Keep covered.
5. While the urad is cooking, soak the dried fenugreek leaves in a bowl of cold water. (Gently rub the dried leaves in the water to release any loose soil that may have stuck to the leaves.)
6. Ten minutes before use, carefully lift the soaked fenugreek leaves from the top of the bowl. (Try not to disturb the dirt that may have settled at the bottom of the bowl.) Place the leaves on kitchen paper to dry.
7. Heat the ghee, add the fenugreek leaves and, stirring continuously, fry to a crispness for about 5 minutes.
8. Pour this *tarka* over the cooked dal, gently mix it in and serve hot.

Serving suggestion

A delicious dal to be served as an accompaniment to a main course, or as a separate course with plain paranthas (page 213).

⬦•⊂⊃•⬦

Chickpea Delight
Kabli Channe ka Maza

White chickpeas have been used in Indian and Middle Eastern cooking for a very long time. In this recipe I have mixed them with roasted ground cumin seed and rock salt. This rock salt is different from the salt available in stores which is refined crystals of the rock salt. This salt smells highly of sulphur and has a distinct taste, which is enhanced further by adding tamarind and other spices.

Serves 4–6
Preparation time: 30 minutes plus 12 hours soaking
Cooking time: 2¹/₂ hours (or less in a pressure cooker)

225g/8 oz white chickpeas
1 litre/1³/₄ pints water
1 teaspoon bicarbonate of
 soda
³/₄ teaspoon salt
50g/2 oz tamarind pulp
2 green chillies
5cm/2-inch piece of fresh
 ginger

1 teaspoon cumin seeds
¹/₂ teaspoon chilli powder
1¹/₂ teaspoons garam masala
2 tablespoons chopped
 coriander leaves
¹/₄ teaspoon rock salt
 (unrefined)
2 tablespoons oil

1. Clean the chickpeas and soak them in plenty of cold water for at least 12 hours.
2. Drain, then wash in a couple of changes of water. Place in a saucepan with the water, bicarbonate of soda and salt.

(Or place in a pressure cooker with two-thirds of the quantity of water and cook for at least 30 minutes at full pressure. Also follow the manufacturer's instructions.)

3. Bring to the boil, then reduce the heat to medium and continue boiling gently until the peas are tender but still retain their shape.

4. Soak the tamarind in warm water for about 20 minutes. Squeeze with your fingers to release the pulp. Strain the juice and reserve. Discard the fibres and seeds.

5. Finely chop the green chillies. Peel and cut the ginger into thin julienne strips.

6. Sprinkle cumin seeds on to a dry frying pan, turn on the heat and, stirring constantly, roast the seeds to a dark colour. (Care must be taken not to burn them.)

7. Transfer the seeds to a dry surface and crush to a coarse powder with a rolling pin or in a pestle and mortar.

8. To the bowl containing the tamarind juice, add the chillies, ginger, chilli powder, garam masala, cumin seeds, coriander leaves and rock salt. Stir well and let it stand for 10–15 minutes.

9. Strain the boiled chickpeas (reserve the liquid for soup).

10. Heat the oil, add the boiled strained chickpeas and, stirring continuously, fry them over high heat for about 5 minutes.

11. Pour in the tamarind mixture and continue frying and tossing the chickpeas about for another 5 minutes until they are well coated with the mixture.

12. Transfer to a serving dish and serve.

Serving suggestion
A versatile dish which can be served as a hot starter, as a separate course with poori (page 224), or as part of the main course. I have also found it delicious when served cold as a summer salad.

Rice

Traditional rice recipes such as *biriyanis* and *pillaus* have been omitted in this chapter. Instead I have created recipes with a fresh taste using ingredients such as smoky bacon, salmon, fenugreek leaves and coriander leaves. Spicing has been kept to a minimum so that nothing masks the true flavour and delicate aroma of the basmati rice and added ingredients.

Coriander rice is unique in this chapter; the method in fact is Mexican, in which the rice is not washed but picked over, and fried first then cooked in milk and water. A delicious concoction. The associated ingredients delicately add colour to the rice, and there are no harsh overtones due to overspicing. Most of the rice dishes have been created to blend with the meats, poultry, fish, vegetables and dals described in the rest of the book.

Rice was first grown in India and south east Asia around 3000 BC and later spread to China and Japan. There are several varieties of rice and the size and thickness of the grain determines the quality and taste of the prepared dish. Basmati rice, which is the long-grained, crescent-shaped grain, is sometimes left to mature for as long as fifteen years before it is used. This rice is most commonly used in the preparation of pillaus and biriyanis. Patna rice, which is long-grained and slightly rounded, is usually used for everyday preparations.

In Indian cookery rice must never be cooked to such an extent that it becomes a soggy mass and sticks together. The rice should be light and fluffy and each grain should be separate. The success of perfectly cooked rice depends on four things: the number of times the rice has been washed, the length of time it has been soaked in water, the amount of water that has been added to it and the temperature at which it is cooked.

Rice should be carefully washed in several changes of water until the water runs clear. It should then be left to soak for no more than 15 to 20 minutes. The length of time that rice has soaked for will often (especially in the case of patna rice) determine the amount of water needed to cook it to perfection. Normally it is believed that the ratio is one to two, i.e. one cup of rice to two cups of water. I find that the ratio can overcook the rice, especially if it has soaked for some time. My method of measuring the amount of water needed for cooking is a very simple one. The soaked rice is drained, placed in a heavy-bottomed saucepan and levelled. Then the water is added carefully. I then dip my clean index finger into the water so that the tip of the finger touches the top of the rice. If the water reaches the first joint on the finger the rice will cook to perfection. Cover the saucepan with a tight-fitting lid, bring to the boil, reduce the heat to a very low setting and leave it to cook for 15 minutes or so until the rice is tender.

The other method which is most commonly used is to quick-boil the rice in plenty of water, then strain it (the starch

183

is used for starching clothes). Sometimes it is rinsed in cold
water and reheated.

⬅━●━➡

Plain Boiled Rice
Sade Uble hue Chawal

Most supermarkets now offer such a baffling choice of rice that
it can be quite difficult to decide which type to buy. To my
mind, the simplest way to make perfectly boiled rice is to buy
patna or long-grain or basmati rice and then proceed as
follows.

Serves 4
Preparation time: 10 minutes plus 30 minutes soaking
Cooking time: 20 minutes

275g/10 oz rice
$^1/_2$ teaspoon salt
Enough water to come 2.5cm/1 inch over the top of rice

1. Thoroughly wash the rice, then soak it in plenty of cold
   water for 30 minutes.
2. Drain the rice, place it in a pan, add the salt and water, mix
   well, bring to the boil, then reduce the heat, cover with
   a tight-fitting lid and gently simmer for about 20 minutes
   until the rice is tender and all the water has evaporated.
3. Lightly fluff up the rice with a fork and serve hot.

Coriander Rice
Dhania Wale Chawal

While on holiday with some friends, Asha and Raj, in the heart of Devon, Asha cooked us a lovely Mexican meal. The rice that she cooked was so interesting that I decided to cook it in the same manner but using my favourite Indian herb – coriander leaves.

Serves 4
Preparation time: 10 minutes
Cooking time: 30 minutes

225g/8 oz basmati rice
50g/2 oz oil or ghee
$^{1}/_{2}$ teaspoon salt
Chilli powder to taste
50g/2 oz fresh coriander
   leaves, finely chopped

4 tablespoons milk
450ml/$^{3}/_{4}$ pint (approx.)
   water

1. Remove any unhusked rice. Place the rice on a clean teatowel and rub it thoroughly clean, taking care not to break up the grains. This method of cleaning will remove any surplus white powder that sticks to the rice. (It is important that the rice is not washed at all, as this would make it stick to the pan when fried.)
2. Heat the oil or ghee, and as soon as it is hot add the rice.
3. Stirring continuously with a metal spoon, fry the rice until it is a lovely golden brown.
4. Remove from heat, add the salt, chilli powder, finely chopped fresh coriander leaves and milk.
5. Place the saucepan back on the heat and give the ingredients a good stir. As soon as the rice has been coated

with the milk, add enough water to come 2.5cm/1 inch over the top of the rice.

6. Reduce the heat and let the rice cook gently until all the water has been absorbed and the rice is tender.
7. Leave the rice in the pan for a few seconds before serving.

Garnish

A delicious garnish which complements this rice is large green chillies slit lengthwise on one side and then stuffed with thin slices of Cheddar cheese. These stuffed chillies should be placed on top of the rice at least 5 minutes before the end of cooking time. This will melt the cheese a little and steam the chillies. Serve one chilli per person.

Serving suggestion

As the dish already has a very interesting flavour, I find it best served with something simple.

❧

Spinach Rice
Chawal Palak Wale

The combination of white and green always looks very attractive and appetizing. Here I have mixed together lightly spiced spinach purée with rice to give a perfect match of colour and taste.

Serves 4–6
Preparation time: 25 minutes plus 30 minutes soaking
Cooking time: 45 minutes

275g/10 oz basmati rice
2 tablespoons ghee
1/2 teaspoon cumin seeds
225g/8 oz frozen spinach
 purée, thawed
1 teaspoon salt
1/2 teaspoon chilli powder

Enough water to come
 2.5cm/1 inch above the
 rice
1 medium onion, finely
 sliced
2.5cm/1 inch fresh ginger,
 finely sliced

1. Thoroughly wash the rice then soak it in plenty of cold water for 30 minutes.
2. Heat 1 tablespoon of the ghee, add the cumin seeds and, as soon as they pop, add the thawed spinach purée, salt and chilli powder. Stir well, reduce the heat, cover and cook for 15–20 minutes until all the moisture from the spinach has dried up.
3. Drain the rice, add it to the spinach, stir-fry for a few minutes then level the rice.
4. Pour in the water, reduce the heat, cover and leave to cook for about 20 minutes until the rice is tender and the moisture completely absorbed.
5. Heat the remaining ghee and add the onion and ginger. Stir-fry to a crisp golden colour and sprinkle this over the rice. Serve at once.

Serving suggestion
Excellent when served with a meat or poultry dish and plain yogurt.

◆━◑◎◐━◆

Green Chilli Rice
Hari Mirch ke Chawal

Green chillies, although they look innocent and appetizing, can be quite lethal inside. It is the seeds more than the shiny green skin that cause the tears to come to one's eyes, yet the flavour of the skin is most inviting. In this recipe, I have removed all the seeds and the stalks, washed the chillies, minced them and cooked them with the rice. This adds not only the beautiful green colour but also a subtle flavour. Remember to wash your hands with soap after handling chillies of any sort.

Serves 4
Preparation time: 20 minutes plus 30 minutes soaking
Cooking time: 20 minutes

275g/10 oz basmati rice
2 green chillies
$^{1}/_{2}$ teaspoon salt
1 tablespoon ghee

$^{1}/_{2}$ teaspoon cumin seeds
Enough water to come
2.5cm/1 inch above the rice

1. Thoroughly wash the rice then soak it in plenty of cold water for about 30 minutes.
2. Remove the stalks and seeds from the chillies and mince or grind them to a fine paste with the salt.
3. Drain the rice.
4. Heat the ghee, add the cumin seeds and, as soon as they pop, add rice and minced chillies.
5. Stir-fry for a couple of minutes then level the rice in the pan.
6. Pour in the water. Cover with a tight-fitting lid, reduce the heat and allow to cook for about 20 minutes, until all the moisture has been absorbed and the rice is tender.
7. Gently fork up the rice right to the bottom of the pan and transfer to a serving dish.

Serving suggestion
Serve hot either with a main meal or as a salad. Those who are feeling brave could garnish with split green chillies.

Rice Flavoured with Curry Leaf
Curry Patte ke Chawal

Curry leaves must never be confused with bay leaves. The two leaves have nothing in common, the first being small and fine with a very distinct curry-like flavour, the second being larger and coarser with a very mild and subtle flavour. Curry leaves can now be bought fresh in most oriental stores.

Serves 4–6
Preparation time: 10 minutes plus 30 minutes soaking
Cooking time: 25 minutes

275g/10 oz basmati rice
1 tablespoon oil
$^1/_2$ teaspoon mustard seeds
2–3 small whole red chillies

5–6 fresh curry leaves
Enough water to reach
  2.5cm/1 inch above the
  rice

1. Thoroughly wash the rice then soak it in plenty of cold water for 30 minutes.
2. Heat the oil, add the mustard seeds and, as soon as they pop, add the red chillies and curry leaves. Cook for a few seconds.
3. Drain the rice, add it to the curry leaf mixture, then stir-fry for a minute and level it.
4. Pour in the water, reduce the heat, cover and cook until the rice is tender and all the moisture has dried up. This should take about 20 minutes.
5. Gently fork up the rice and transfer it to a serving dish. Serve hot immediately.

Serving suggestion
Serve with any main meal, especially one containing a plain pulse and vegetable dish.

Fresh Ginger Pillau
Adrak ka Pillau

Fortunately fresh ginger is now available in almost all the supermarkets and, of course, in oriental stores. Ginger keeps well in a cool place and, if sliced, ground or shredded, can be frozen in ice-cube trays. Use one cube at a time when required.

Serves 4–6
Preparation time: 20 minutes plus 30 minutes soaking
Cooking time: 25 minutes

275g/10 oz basmati rice
7.5cm/3-inch piece of fresh
  ginger
1 medium onion
2 tablespoons ghee
$1/2$ teaspoon cumin seeds

$1/2$ teaspoon salt
Enough water to reach
  2.5cm/1 inch above the
  rice
$1/4$ teaspoon chilli powder

1. Thoroughly wash the rice and soak it in clean water for 30 minutes.
2. Scrape off the thin skin from the ginger. Divide into two pieces, one about 5cm/2 inches long and the other shorter. Finely grate or mince the large piece of ginger and squeeze out the juice. Reserve the juice, discard the ginger pulp. Finely slice the other piece of ginger.
3. Finely slice the onion. Heat 1 tablespoon of the ghee and add the onion and cumin seeds. Stir-fry to a rich golden colour.
4. Drain the rice, wash once again in clear water and add it to the browned onion. Pour in the ginger juice, add the salt and stir-fry for a minute or two.
5. Level the rice, then pour in the water. Reduce the heat,

cover and allow to cook for about 20 minutes until tender and all the moisture has been absorbed.

6. Gently fork up the rice, working your way to the bottom, and transfer on to a serving dish.
7. In a small pan heat the remaining ghee, add the sliced ginger and, stirring frequently, fry to a crisp golden colour. Add the chilli powder, stir-fry for a second or two, then pour the crisp ginger on top of the rice. Serve immediately.

Serving suggestion
Serve as an accompaniment to the main meal, consisting of dal and vegetables.

⊨◦⊨

Delicious Ajowan Rice
Ajowan ke Sawadi Chawal

Ajowan is a hot spice, but emits a heat different from that of either chilli or the other hot spices, e.g. cloves, cinnamon, cardamoms etc. It blends extremely well with lemon or lime juice as in this recipe where celery sticks are lightly sautéed in ghee to enhance the flavour of the rice.

Serves 4
Preparation time: 20 minutes plus 30 minutes soaking
Cooking time: 30 minutes

275g/10 oz basmati rice
3 sticks of celery plus leaves
1 tablespoon oil
1 teaspoon ajowan seeds
3/4 teaspoon salt

1 1/2 tablespoons lemon juice
Enough water to come
  2.5cm/1 inch above the
  rice

1. Thoroughly wash the rice then soak it in plenty of cold

191

water for about 30 minutes. Wash the celery sticks, remove the leaves and keep them aside for garnishing.

2. Cut the celery sticks into 5cm/2-inch long julienne strips.
3. Immerse the leaves in cold water to rejuvenate them.
4. Heat the oil, add the ajowan seeds and, as soon as they pop and splutter, add the celery strips and stir-fry for a few minutes.
5. Drain the rice and add it to the celery along with the salt and lemon juice. Stir-fry for another minute then level the rice.
6. Pour over the water. Cover with a tight-fitting lid, reduce the heat and cook until the rice is tender and all the moisture has dried up. This will take about 20 minutes.
7. Gently fork up the rice right to the bottom and transfer it to a bread tin. Pack the rice in firmly, then quickly invert the tin over a serving dish. Tap on top and ease the tin away to reveal a perfectly shaped rice tin. Garnish with the celery leaves.

Serving suggestion
Serve hot with the main meal.

❦

Mustard Rice
Rai aur Chawal

Mustard cress is seldom included in Indian cooking, although the pungent mustard seed is used all over the country, not only as a spice but also for its oil, and the leaves as a vegetable. In this recipe I have used the pungent mustard seeds to flavour the rice, adding mustard cress right at the end to give it colour and a fresh flavour.

Serves 4
Preparation time: 10 minutes plus 30 minutes soaking
Cooking time: 25 minutes

275g/10 oz basmati rice
1 tablespoon oil
1 teaspoon mustard seeds
1/2 teaspoon salt

Enough water to reach
2.5cm/1 inch above the
rice
1 container mustard cress

1. Thoroughly wash the rice then soak it in plenty of cold
   water for about 30 minutes.
2. Drain the rice.
3. Heat the oil, add the mustard seeds and, as soon as they
   pop and splutter, add the rice. Stir well then fry the rice
   for a few minutes and level it.
4. Add the salt and water. Reduce the heat, cover with a
   tight-fitting lid and allow to cook for about 20 minutes
   until the rice is tender and all the moisture has dried up.
5. Snip the mustard cress from its container, place in a
   colander and wash under cold running water. Shake dry,
   sprinkle on to the rice and carefully and gently fork it into
   the rice to mix completely.

Serving suggestion
Serve this hot as part of the main meal, or cold as a salad.

Salmon Rice
Salmon Wale Chawal

A recipe created by pure accident, when unthinkingly I added
a container full of pink salmon from the fridge instead of the
container sitting next to it. The result was so delicious that it
has become a favourite exotic dish. The only spice flavouring
is aniseed.

Serves 4
Preparation time: 20 minutes plus 30 minutes soaking
Cooking time: 25 minutes

275g/10 oz basmati rice
1 225g/8-oz can pink salmon
1 tablespoon ghee
2 teaspoons lightly crushed
    aniseeds
½ teaspoon salt
¼ teaspoon freshly ground
    black pepper
Enough water to reach
    2.5cm/1 inch above the
    rice

1. Thoroughly wash the rice, then soak it in plenty of cold water for about 30 minutes.
2. Cut the salmon into small pieces.
3. Drain the rice.
4. Heat the ghee, add the aniseed, stir-fry for a minute then add the salmon. Fry for another minute then add the rice, salt and pepper.
5. Stir-fry for another minute to mix the spice and salmon with the rice. Level the rice off.
6. Pour in the water, reduce the heat, cover and cook for about 20 minutes until the rice is tender and all the moisture has dried up.
7. Gently fluff up the rice with a fork, working right down to the bottom of the pan.
8. Transfer the rice to a fish mould. Then carefully invert it on to a serving dish. Tap the mould to loosen the rice and serve.

Serving suggestion
Serve hot as part of a main course which includes a light vegetable and pulse dish, to emphasize the delicate flavour of salmon. Or serve cold as a salad.

Spicy Prawn Rice
Masaledar Jhinga Chawal

Although I have used prawns in this recipe you can substitute any shellfish such as lobster, crab, mussels and even oysters.

Serves 4
Preparation time: 25 minutes plus 1 hour marinating plus 30 minutes soaking
Cooking time: 25 minutes

Small slice of fresh ginger
1 clove of garlic
100g/4 oz frozen prawns
1 teaspoon garam masala
1 teaspoon salt
1/4 teaspoon chilli powder

2 tablespoons lemon juice
275g/10 oz basmati rice
Enough water to reach
   2.5cm/1 inch above the
   rice

1. Finely mince the ginger and garlic. Place the prawns, ginger, garlic, garam masala, salt, chilli powder and lemon juice in a bowl. Mix well, cover and leave in a cool place to marinate for about 1 hour.
2. Thoroughly wash the rice then soak it in plenty of cold water for about 30 minutes.
3. Drain the rice then put it in a heavy-bottomed saucepan, add the marinated prawns and all the marinade. Mix thoroughly, level the rice.
4. Pour in the water. Cover, reduce the heat and leave to cook for about 25 minutes until all the moisture has dried up and the rice is tender.
5. Gently fork up the rice right to the bottom and transfer it to a serving dish.

Serving suggestion
As the dish is rich enough on its own, it is best served with a dal and crisp ginger in yogurt (page 208).

❖◦❖

Bacon-flavoured Rice
Chawal aur Bacon ka Mail

Smoked bacon, a very recent addition to Indian cuisine, lends a unique flavour to rice.

Serves 4
Preparation time: 20 minutes plus 15 minutes soaking
Cooking time: 35 minutes

275g/10 oz long-grain rice
225g/8 oz smoked bacon
8 black peppercorns,
  coarsely crushed

$^1/_2$ teaspoon salt
Enough water to reach about
  2.5cm/1inch above the
  rice

1. Thoroughly wash the rice, then soak it for about 15 minutes before draining.
2. Remove the rind and any bone from the bacon. Divide it into two portions, then cut one half into small 1cm/$^1/_2$-inch pieces and the other half into long 1cm/$^1/_2$-inch wide strips.
3. Heat up a heavy-based saucepan, add the bacon pieces and strips and, stirring frequently, fry the bacon to a crisp golden colour.
4. Carefully remove the bacon strips and drain them on kitchen paper.
5. Add the rice, coarsely crushed black pepper and salt. Stir to mix all the ingredients.
6. Level the rice then pour in the water. Cover with a

tight-fitting lid, reduce the heat and allow to cook until all the moisture has evaporated and the rice is tender.

7. Gently fluff up the rice with a fork and transfer on to a serving dish.
8. Garnish with crispy fried bacon strips.

Serving suggestion
As the flavour of bacon is quite unique, serve it as an accompaniment to a less elaborate dish.

Yogurt

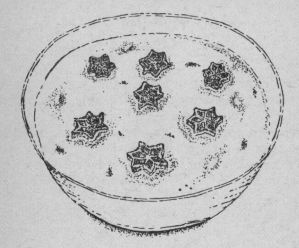

A firmly set bowl of yogurt is so appetizing that at times I feel it a shame to spoil its natural flavour and texture. But as most of us are never satisfied with sameness at every mealtime, I have created some *raitas* or yogurt salads that can be served not only as a dish to be enjoyed on its own but also as part of the accompaniment to other dishes. Yogurt has been in existence since before recorded history and a brief outline of its development is given on pages 46–8 where I also give the method for making yogurt at home. It is a fascinating food which lends itself to a variety of dishes both sweet and savoury.

I have created new combinations with yogurt such as shredded chicken, crisply fried pork, roasted red and green peppers to name a few. All these interesting ingredients not only enhance the unique taste of yogurt but also create a different texture. A mouthful of natural yogurt with crunchy fried okra will be a dish to remember.

⚊

Crisp-fried Pork Raita
Karare Maans ka Raita

The idea for this recipe originated one evening when I was cooking some Chinese food. The dish contained crisply fried thin strips of pork, which are then mixed with other vegetables. On an impulse I added some of the crisply fried strips of pork to the already chilled yogurt and served it at once. The reaction from the guests was worth the impulsive change in menu.

Serves 4
Preparation time: 25 minutes plus 30 minutes chilling
Cooking time: 10 minutes

75g/3 oz tender loin of pork
  or beef
³/₄ teaspoon salt
600ml/1 pint natural yogurt

1 tablespoon finely chopped
  coriander leaves
3 tablespoons oil
2 whole dried red chillies

1. Remove any excess fat from the tender loin. Cut into matchstick-thin strips. (A lengthy process but well worth it.)
2. Sprinkle a little of the salt on to the pork strips and mix it in with your fingers. Leave aside for 5 minutes.
3. Lightly whip the yogurt to a smooth consistency. Add the rest of the salt and the coriander leaves. Mix well and chill while the pork is being fried.

199

4. Heat the oil in a *karahi* or heavy-bottomed frying pan to smoking point.
5. Stand well back in case of spluttering and add the salted pork strips and red chillies. Fry, stirring continuously, to a crisp golden colour – this must be done over high heat.
6. Drain on kitchen paper for a minute then add at once to the chilled yogurt. Mix in and serve at once.

Serving suggestion
As with the chicken *raita*, serve this on its own with a main meal of rice, dal and/or vegetables.

⊷⊶⊷

Spiced Liver in Yogurt
Kaleji ka Raita

The hunting lodge belonging to His Highness Arvind Singh of Udaipur is one of those tranquil places where the mind and body feel at their most peaceful. During my stay there a whole variety of dishes was prepared by the chefs, but the most unusual and delicious was this *Kaleji ka Raita*.

Serves 4
Preparation time: 10 minutes
Cooking time: 15 minutes

100g/4 oz lamb liver	600ml/1 pint water
4 black peppercorns	600ml/1 pint natural yogurt
1 green cardamom	1 teaspoon salt
Small piece of cinnamon	$^1/_2$ teaspoon freshly ground
1 bay leaf	black pepper
$^1/_2$ teaspoon cumin seeds	1 tablespoon freshly
2 cloves	chopped coriander leaves

1. Remove any gristle from the liver.
2. Tie in a piece of muslin the peppercorns, cardamom, cinnamon, bay leaf, cumin seeds and cloves. Place this in a saucepan with the water.
3. Bring to the boil, reduce the heat and simmer for 10 minutes to reduce the quantity by half.
4. Add the liver and simmer for another 5 minutes. Remove the liver and allow to cool. Discard the water and spice bag.
5. When the liver is completely cold, cut it into small cubes.
6. Lightly whip the yogurt then add the liver, salt and black pepper. Mix thoroughly.
7. Sprinkle with the coriander leaves.
8. Chill thoroughly before serving.

Serving suggestion
Forms an excellent starter to a meal: serve in small ramekin dishes. Or it could be an accompaniment to an otherwise plain meal.

Chicken in Yogurt
Murghi ka Raita

Highly spiced shredded chicken is used in this unusual yogurt *raita*. The chicken breast is simmered gently in an aromatic stock, cooled, shredded and added to the chilled yogurt with finely chopped green chilli. A delicious and satisfying dish.

Serves 4–6
Preparation time: 20 minutes
Cooking time: 25 minutes plus 30 minutes chilling

4 black peppercorns
1 small whole red chilli
2 cloves
Small stick of cinnamon
1 black cardamom
1/2 teaspoon cumin seeds
1/2 teaspoon coriander seeds

450ml/3/4 pint water
1 teaspoon salt
100g/4 oz chicken breast, skinned
600ml/1 pint natural yogurt
1 green chilli

1. In a piece of muslin tie the first seven ingredients.
2. Add this spice bag to a saucepan containing the water, half the salt and the chicken breast.
3. Cover and bring to the boil, then reduce the heat and allow to simmer gently for about 25 minutes until the chicken is tender.
4. Remove from the stock. (Reserve the stock for later use.) Discard the spice bag.
5. Allow the chicken to cool, then, using your fingers, shred it into long strips.
6. Lightly whip the yogurt to a smooth consistency. Add the chicken shreds and the remaining salt. Stir well and chill for half an hour.
7. Finely slice the chilli and sprinkle on top just before serving. (If a milder chilli taste is required, split the chilli, remove its seeds, rub a little salt on the inside and rinse thoroughly.)

Serving suggestion
Serve slightly chilled along with the main course, which, of course, should not contain another poultry dish. I also like to serve this as a starter with crisp deep-fried chappati triangles.

Note: These deep-fried chappati triangles must not be confused with deep-fried poori (page 224). The chappati triangles are made of leftover chappatis that have hardened overnight, are cut into triangles and deep-fried to golden crispness.

Spinach in Yogurt
Palak ka Raita

Whenever I see tender young spinach leaves I simply cannot wait to get them home and make two of my favourite dishes. One is the spinach and egg bake on page 159 and the other is this particular dish. Although it may sound an unusual combination, I can assure you it is delicious.

Serves 4
Preparation time: 20 minutes
Cooking time: 10–15 minutes

225g/8 oz fresh tender
  spinach
3 tablespoons water
1 medium onion
1 green chilli

1 clove of garlic
1 tablespoon oil
600ml/1 pint natural yogurt
1 teaspoon salt
Freshly ground black pepper

1. Discard from the spinach any tough stems and soggy leaves. Place the tender spinach leaves in a saucepan with the water and bring quickly to the boil. Then reduce the heat and simmer gently for 5–6 minutes until the leaves are tender.
2. Remove and drain thoroughly. Gently squeeze any excess moisture from the leaves and chop them roughly.
3. Finely chop the onion and green chilli and crush the garlic.
4. Heat the oil, add the onion and sauté for a few minutes until it is soft and transparent but not browned. Add the spinach and sauté for another few minutes.
5. Lightly whip the yogurt and spoon it into a serving bowl. Add the salt, green chilli, garlic, black pepper and the sautéed spinach and onion mixture.
6. Mix thoroughly and chill before serving.

Serving suggestion
An excellent dish to serve with a plain dal and chappatis (page 211).

❧

Crispy Okra in Yogurt
Talihui Bhindi ka Raita

Okra, or ladies' fingers, are now available just about everywhere, including most supermarkets. For this dish buy only the very firm okra, because if they are limp they will absorb too much oil while frying.

Serves 4
Preparation time: 15 minutes
Cooking time: 10 minutes

600ml/1 pint natural yogurt
100g/4 oz fresh crisp okra
Oil for deep-frying
1 teaspoon salt
½ teaspoon chilli powder
1 teaspoon roasted cumin powder

1. Lightly whip the yogurt and spoon it into a serving bowl.
2. Wash the okra and dry thoroughly with a clean cloth or kitchen paper.
3. Cut off the stalk ends and slice the okra into very thin slices no more than 3mm/⅓ inch thick.
4. Heat the oil to near-smoking point. Carefully sprinkle a handful of the sliced okra on to the hot oil. These should fry to a crisp golden colour in a few seconds.
5. Lift out with a perforated spoon. Drain on kitchen paper.
6. Repeat until all the okra are fried.

7. Add the salt and chilli and cumin powder to the yogurt. Mix well.
8. Sprinkle fried okra on top of the yogurt just before serving. (Do not mix, as it looks attractive just forming a layer on the top.)

Serving suggestion
Serve as part of the main meal.

⊷•⊶

Roasted Peppers in Yogurt Sauce
Bhoni Mirch Dahi me

Roasted or scorched pimentoes acquire a unique taste all their own, quite unmatched by anything else that I have tasted.

Serves 4
Preparation and cooking time: 25 minutes

2 green peppers
2 red peppers
600ml/1 pint natural yogurt
Freshly ground black pepper
1 teaspoon salt

1 tablespoon oil
1/2 teaspoon mustard seeds
1 tablespoon freshly
  chopped coriander leaves

1. Wash and wipe dry the peppers. Place a wire rack over a naked gas flame or electric ring. (If a rack is not available, place the peppers under a hot grill.) Place the peppers on the rack and roast them thoroughly on all sides until the skin is charred.
2. In the meantime lightly whip the yogurt and add the freshly ground black pepper and salt. Mix thoroughly.
3. Remove the peppers from the rack or from under the grill once they are charred. Let them cool for a few minutes then carefully scrape off the charred skin. Cut into

quarters. Discard the seeds and stalks. (If the peppers are large, cut them into eighths.)
4. Add the cut peppers to the yogurt. Leave to chill for a little while before serving.
5. Just before serving, heat the oil and, when hot, add the mustard seeds. They should pop at once. Pour this over the peppers. Sprinkle some finely chopped coriander leaves on top and serve.

Serving suggestion
This delicious *raita* can either be served as part of the main meal or as a starter with some thin slices of toast.

❦

Roasted Aubergines in Yogurt
Bhoone Baingan ka Raita

The aroma of aubergines being roasted over charcoal is something quite unique. Unfortunately most homes don't have the facility of live charcoal in their kitchens, however aubergines can be roasted quite successfully over a naked gas flame or under a very hot electric grill. The skin is removed and the aubergine is added to the lightly whipped yogurt, sprinkled with roasted ground cumin and served chilled.

Serves 4
Preparation time: 10 minutes
Cooking time: 15–20 minutes plus 30 minutes chilling

1 medium-sized round aubergine
600ml/1 pint natural yogurt
1½ teaspoons cumin seeds
1 teaspoon salt

½ teaspoon freshly ground black pepper
1 tablespoon finely chopped coriander leaves

1. Wash and wipe the aubergine. Place it on top of a naked gas or charcoal flame or under a hot electric grill. Turning frequently, ensure that the skin is charred on all sides. (This will also cook the aubergine.)
2. Once the skin is completely charred, remove from the fire and allow to cool for a few minutes. Then carefully (because of any steam trapped inside the aubergine) peel off all the charred skin. Cut off the stalk.
3. Place the roasted aubergine in a bowl and, with a fork, mash it up completely, so that the flesh is broken and does not stick together.
4. Lightly whip the yogurt to a smooth consistency. Add the mashed aubergine, stir well, cover and allow to chill for at least half an hour.
5. Place the cumin seeds in a frying pan and dry-roast to a dark colour. Keep stirring continuously until the seeds start spluttering and emitting a very distinct aroma.
6. Remove from the heat and place the seeds on a rolling board or in an electric spice-grinder or in a pestle and mortar. Crush them to a fine powder.
7. Sprinkle the salt, pepper, cumin and coriander leaves on to the chilled yogurt and aubergine.
8. Stir well, and serve.

Serving suggestion
An excellent chilled starter served with yesterday's chappatis (page 213), or as a yogurt accompaniment to the main course.

Crisp Ginger in Yogurt
Adrak ka Raita

This dish, I must confess, happened by mistake. While preparing the ginger *tarka* for a dal that I had made, I accidentally poured the crisply fried ginger *tarka* on the yogurt that was in a dish alongside the dal. As I couldn't remove the ginger from the yogurt, I just prayed that my dinner party would not be ruined because of one dish. Imagine my delight when everyone praised to the skies this crispy ginger *raita*. It has now become a favourite.

Serves 4
Preparation time: 10 minutes
Cooking time: 5 minutes

5cm/2-inch piece of fresh ginger
600ml/1 pint natural yogurt
1 tablespoon ghee
$\frac{1}{2}$ teaspoon salt
$\frac{1}{2}$ teaspoon freshly ground black pepper

1. Scrape the skin from the ginger. Cut into very fine julienne strips.
2. Lightly whip the yogurt and pour it into a chilled serving bowl.
3. Heat the ghee, add the ginger and fry to a crisp brown colour. (Care must be taken not to overbrown as that will ruin the delicate flavour of fresh ginger.)
4. Add the fried ginger to the yogurt along with the salt and pepper.
5. Serve at once, otherwise the ginger will become soggy and lose its appeal.

Serving suggestion
Ideal combination with a meat or poultry dish which is baked and has no sauce. Serve either chappati (page 211) or rice (page 184) with it.

Breads

Almost all of north India simply lives on bread, not the Western sliced loaf but a wholemeal, freshly baked unleavened bread called chappati, which is rich in fibre. Chappati, the lightest version of bread anywhere in the world, has been underrated by most non-Indian authors of books on bread. Chappatis have to be baked just before eating as they soon lose their suppleness if left to go cold, and it is normal practice in an Indian household for the lady of the house to dish out hot chappatis to the rest of the family straight from the hot griddle on to their plates.

Paranthas, although made from the same soft dough, are richer as a small amount of clarified butter – ghee – is incorporated in the rolling and folding and then they are shallow-fried. They are excellent for freezing in batches; just right for an emergency.

Stuffed paranthas are a favourite all over India, and I have created some delicious new stuffings, such as soft cheese – paneer – spicy boiled chicken, baby shrimps or just mint to flavour the bread.

Pooris – the puffed wholemeal rounds that are deep-fried – are not recommended for people who are weight-conscious or worried about cholesterol. A delicious deep-fried version of chappatis, these definitely have to be eaten while hot, and can be stuffed with a variety of fillings.

A few plain flour breads such as nan are also very popular but usually cooked either in the restaurants or for special occasions because the special *tandoor* oven is required. Although a sort of substitute can be made in the oven, the unique taste and texture is missing. This is one of the few breads that is leavened – with yeast or soured yogurt. Nan is excellent for freezing: it can be reheated under a hot grill in just a minute or so.

❧

Wholemeal Bread
Chappati or *Roti*

Chappati is by far the most popular bread because of its lightness and easy digestibility. The method of making chappatis can be perfected with a little bit of practice

Serves 4
Preparation time: 15 minutes plus 15 minutes resting
Cooking time: 15–20 minutes

225g/8 oz wholemeal flour
150ml/¼ pint tepid water
A little ghee or butter

1. Place the flour in a bowl and to it add the water a little at a time in order to bind the flour.
2. Once all the flour has been absorbed, place the dough on a clean surface and knead it thoroughly. The easiest method is to shape your hand into a fist and then press the dough down firmly on to the surface, turning the dough over after a few kneadings.
3. Once the dough feels fairly soft and pliable (the consistency should be that of shortcrust pastry), remove it from the surface and return it to the bowl. Cover it with a lid or a piece of damp cloth. Leave it to rest for at least 15 minutes.
4. Heat a frying pan, griddle or *tava*. Break off a small piece of dough no larger than the size of a ping-pong ball and shape it into a smooth ball between the palms of your hands.

5. Dip this ball into some dry flour in order to coat it. Place it on a clean surface and roll it out into a thin round no more than 3mm/^{1}/$_8$ inch thick and about 12.5cm/5 inches in diameter. If the chappati tends to stick to the rolling surface, carefully lift it up and dip it into the dry flour once more.
6. Carefully place the rolled-out chappati on to the hot *tava* or frying pan. As soon as the top side becomes transparent and small bubbles start to appear on the surface, turn it over, and repeat the process. At this stage take a clean teatowel and carefully press down the edges of the chappati. This process will not only make sure that the edges are cooked but also make the chappati puff up, so ensuring that the texture is light and fluffy. As soon as both sides of the chappati have brown spots on the surface, the chappati is cooked.
7. Remove it from the hot griddle or frying pan and smear with a little ghee or butter. Serve at once. If that is not possible then keep them wrapped up in a clean teatowel or foil.

Freezing hint

Chappatis can be frozen very successfully both cooked or uncooked. If they are frozen uncooked, line them with freezer paper; when needed, thaw them out slightly and cook in the normal way. If they are frozen cooked, there is no need to thaw: place them straight under the hot grill and heat them through for a few minutes.

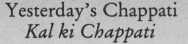

Yesterday's Chappati
Kal ki Chappati

I invariably find that at the end of dinner one or two or sometimes more chappatis are left over. If I haven't frozen them straight away I let them dry out overnight, although still wrapped in a clean cloth. The next day, when they have become slightly hard, divide the chappatis into quarters and deep-fry to a crisp golden brown, drain and allow to cool. Serve them with any of the starters that I have described. These deep-fried chappatis also make excellent crisp snacks.

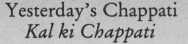

Plain Paranthas
Sade Paranthe

Paranthas are a richer version of the plain chappatis, in that a small amount of fat, i.e. ghee, is incorporated into the folds of the rolled-out chappati, and usually shallow-fried to a delicious crispness. For the figure- and cholesterol-conscious the shallow-frying bit can be omitted, and just a light smear of ghee or butter applied to one side only after the parantha is cooked – but often people disregard all such honest thoughts when eating freshly made paranthas.

Makes about 8
Preparation time: 15 minutes (less in a dough mixer) plus 15 minutes resting
Cooking time: 20–25 minutes

225g/8 oz wholemeal flour   4 tablespoons melted ghee
150ml/¹/₄ pint (approx.)   Bowl of dry flour
   water

1. Place the flour in a bowl, add the water a little at a time and bind into a soft pliable dough. Knead well for at least 10 minutes (less in a mixer). Cover with a damp cloth and leave to rest for at least 15 minutes. (This will help to soften the flour buds and make a softer parantha.)

2. Heat up a *tava* or griddle to a fairly high temperature. (The temperature is correct when a little dry flour sprinkled on to the *tava* burns almost at once.) Pour $1/2$ teaspoon of ghee on to the *tava*, spread it on the surface, and wipe it off with a kitchen paper. (This will prevent the parantha from sticking to the surface.)

3. Break off a small piece of dough about the size of a large walnut. Shape it into a smooth ball between the palms of your hands.

4. Flatten the ball slightly, dip it in some dry flour just to coat the surface. (This prevents it from sticking to the rolling surface.)

5. Roll the dough into a round no more than 10cm/4 inches in diameter. Spread about $1/2$ teaspoon of melted ghee on it. Then fold it up like puff pastry, i.e. fold one-third into the centre, smear a little ghee on that, then fold the other third over the top and smear a little ghee on this. You are now left with a long rectangle of 2.5cm/1 inch × 10cm/4 inches. Fold this rectangle in the same way, up a third and down a third so that you are left with a neat square of 4cm/$1^1/2$ inches × 4cm/$1^1/2$ inches approximately.

6. Dip this square of dough into some dry flour and roll it out into a square no bigger than 12.5cm/5 inches, but still keeping to its square shape.

7. Carefully lift it off the rolling surface and place it on the hot *tava*.

8. Within a few seconds small bubbles will start appearing on the surface and the parantha will become opaque. This is an indication that the underneath side is semi-cooked and ready to be turned over.

9. Use a spatula or your fingers to turn the parantha over to the other side. Repeat the same process once more, only

214

this time small brown spots will have appeared on the underneath side. This means that that side is cooked.

10. Turn the parantha back once more to complete cooking. Using a clean teatowel, gently press down the sides of the parantha on to the *tava*. This will ensure that the edges, which are thicker than the middle, are thoroughly cooked.

11. The brown spots on the underneath side will be more widespread. Remove the cooked parantha from the *tava*, smear a little ghee on the side with fewer brown spots and serve at once or wrap in another teatowel and keep warm.

12. If a crisp parantha is required, smear a little ghee on each side while it is still on the *tava*. Repeat the process twice and then remove and serve hot as this parantha will go limp if left standing around.

Serving suggestion
Serve these paranthas with anything, as they form the staple food like potatoes or pasta in a Western meal.

Alternative suggestion
Different shaped paranthas can be made using the same dough.

Round paranthas
Roll out the round, this time to a diameter of 15cm/6 inches. Smear some ghee all over and, starting at the edge nearest you, roll up the round to give a long rolled-up sausage. Lift up one end of the roll with your right hand. Place the other end in the palm of the left hand and, using the tip as a centre point, wind the rest of the roll around the centre. Press the other end firmly to the side. Lightly flatten the round, dip in dry flour and roll out into a perfect round of about 12.5cm/5 inches. Proceed as for plain paranthas.

Triangular paranthas
Roll out the piece of dough into a round of about 10cm/4

215

inches. Smear a little ghee all over and fold in half. Smear some more ghee on top then fold into quarter. Dip into dry flour and roll out into a triangle. Proceed as for plain paranthas. The uniqueness of these paranthas, no matter what their shape, is that when they have cooked to perfection, you can separate the layers or count the folds, as each layer on which you smeared ghee separates from the next during cooking and incorporates more air.

Freezing hint
Excellent for freezing. Stack them up one on top of the other. Allow to cool down, then wrap in either freezer foil or cling-film, and freeze. The paranthas do not stick to one another. Just slip a knife in between the paranthas, give a sharp twist, and they will separate at once. There is no need to thaw them, just place under a hot grill for a minute or in the microwave (in which case, wrap in a clean teatowel as they tend to harden). Serve immediately.

<hr/>

Chicken Stuffed Paranthas
Murghi ke Paranthe

One such parantha is enough for an average eater, but that should not stop anyone from indulging once in a while. Chicken breast is boiled in a highly spiced stock and shredded, then a combination of herbs and spices is added to make a delicious parantha.

Makes 10
Preparation time: 40 minutes, including 15 minutes resting
Cooking time: 45 minutes

4 black peppercorns	1 clove of garlic
2 cloves	Small piece of ginger
Very small piece of cinnamon	1 green chilli
	1 teaspoon ground cumin
2 green cardamoms	$1/2$ teaspoon garam masala
175g/6 oz chicken breast	1 teaspoon salt
450g/1 lb wholemeal flour	2 tablespoons finely chopped
300ml/$1/2$ pint water	coriander leaves
1 medium onion	3 tablespoons ghee

1. Tie the peppercorns, cloves, cinnamon and cardamoms in a piece of muslin. Skin the chicken breast and place it in a small saucepan along with the spice bag and just enough water to cover the chicken. Simmer this stock gently for about 20 minutes until the chicken is tender.

2. Mix together the flour and water. Bind into a soft dough. Leave to rest for 15 minutes.

3. Remove the chicken breast and allow it to cool, then shred with your fingers into fine strips.

4. Finely chop the onion, crush the garlic and finely chop the ginger and green chilli.

5. Sprinkle the ground cumin, garam masala, salt, onion, ginger, green chilli, garlic and coriander leaves on the shredded chicken. Mix all the ingredients. (It is important that the chicken is absolutely cold, as any moisture will result in an unsatisfactory stuffing.)

6. Divide the dough into 10 equal portions, then halve these portions so that you have 20 small pieces of dough. Shape each piece into a smooth ball then roll out two of the balls into a round of about 10cm/4 inches in diameter.

7. Spread a tablespoon of the mixture on one of the chappatis. Place the other rolled-out chappati on top, press down the edges of the chappati firmly so that the two stick together.

8. Sprinkle a little dry flour on top and then carefully roll it out into a larger round but no more than 12.5cm/5 inches in diameter.

9. Heat a *tava* or griddle, carefully place the stuffed parantha

on it. Allow to cook for a few seconds then carefully turn the parantha over. Smear some ghee on top and allow the underneath side to cook for a few more seconds.

10. Turn the parantha over, smear some more ghee on top and repeat the process once more, so that the parantha is nice and crisp.

11. Remove from the *tava* and serve hot at once.

Serving suggestion
Serve this extremely rich parantha with just plain yogurt as there is no need for any other accompaniment.

❧❧❧

Paranthas Stuffed with Fish
Machchi ke Paranthe

A most interesting stuffing for paranthas.

Makes 10
Preparation time: 30 minutes
Cooking time: 40 minutes

350g/12 oz cod or any other firm white fish
4 black peppercorns
1 bay leaf
2 tablespoons lemon juice
300ml/$^1/_2$ pint (approx.) water
1 medium onion
2.5cm/1 inch piece of ginger
1 clove of garlic
1–2 green chillies
1 teaspoon ground coriander
1 teaspoon ground cumin
1 teaspoon salt
1 tablespoon finely chopped coriander leaves
450g/1 lb wholemeal flour

1. Thoroughly wash the fish, place it along with the black peppercorns, bay leaf, lemon juice and enough water to just cover the fish in a saucepan with a lid. Cover and simmer gently until the fish is tender.

2. Remove the fish, skin and bone it, then mash into small flakes. Allow to cool completely. Squeeze out any excess water.
3. Finely chop the onion, ginger, garlic and green chilli.
4. As soon as the fish has cooled down add the ground coriander and cumin along with the salt and coriander leaves. Mix thoroughly. (It is important to ensure that no excess moisture remains in the fish as that will make the parantha difficult to roll out.)
5. Follow the exact procedure as that for chicken stuffed paranthas.
6. Serve hot at once.

Serving suggestions
Serve hot with tamarind chutney. Excellent for a late sunday brunch.

◄═►◦◄═►

Soft Cheese Stuffed Paranthas
Paneer ke Paranthe

My young daughter loves potato-stuffed paranthas, and no matter how hard I tried to get her to eat paneer, she would just refuse until one day when I tricked her. I stuffed the parantha with a spicy paneer mixture, and as it resembled spiced potatoes she thoroughly enjoyed it and to this day I haven't told her the truth. In this recipe the paneer must be absolutely dry, so drain it well, squeeze out all the excess water by placing the cheese under a heavy object (I use my marble rolling slab), then crumble it into fine powder, mix it with spices and use.

Makes 8
Preparation time: 30 minutes plus 2–3 hours draining
Cooking time: 30 minutes

225g/8 oz wholemeal flour
1 dessertspoon melted ghee
150ml/¼ pint (approx.)
  water
100g/4 oz paneer (page 44)

1 teaspoon salt
1 teaspoon chilli powder
1 teaspoon ground cumin
3 tablespoons ghee

1. Mix together the flour and melted ghee, then add a little water at a time and bind the flour into a soft dough.
2. Cover with a damp cloth and leave to rest for 15 minutes.
3. Make sure the paneer is crumbled very finely. Mix in the salt, chilli powder and the cumin powder.
4. Roll out and fold the parantha like the *podina* parantha (page 221) until the very last fold. Then roll out the round to 10cm/4 inches diameter. Sprinkle some crumbled paneer on to it and carefully roll it up for the last time.
5. Place on a hot *tava* or griddle and proceed as for the *poodina* parantha.

Serving suggestion
Serve this delicious parantha with a dish of chicken in yogurt (page 201).

Freezing hint
Can be frozen successfully but do re-fry just once before serving to achieve that crispness again.

Mint Stuffed Paranthas
Podine ke Paranthe

The Bokhara restaurant in the plush Maurya Hotel in New Delhi boasts an exquisite North West Frontier cuisine, i.e. food from the bordering regions of Afghanistan and Peshawar and part of northernmost Kashmir. It was here at this beautiful restaurant that I ate melt-in-the-mouth *tandoori roti* stuffed with mint and spices. An unforgettable experience. This recipe is adapted to a parantha cooked on the *tava* rather than in the *tandoor*.

Makes 6–8
Preparation time: 15 minutes plus 15 minutes resting
Cooking time: 30 minutes

225g/8 oz wholemeal flour
25g/1 oz plain flour
4 tablespoons melted ghee
1 egg, lightly beaten

Pinch of salt
3 teaspoons dried mint
A little tepid water for
   binding

1. In a bowl combine the two flours, 1 tablespoon of melted ghee, lightly beaten egg, salt and 1 teaspoon of mint.
2. Work the dough with your fingers to get the feel of the consistency. Bind the flour to a soft pliable dough. Add a little tepid water at a time to make the soft dough. Cover with a damp cloth and leave to rest for 10–15 minutes.
3. Divide the dough into 6–8 equal parts. Shape them into smooth balls. Roll out into rounds of no more than 10cm/4 inches in diameter. Smear some ghee on top and fold it up like a round plain parantha. Roll out into a round, smear some more ghee on top and once again roll it up into a long sausage shape. Repeat this twice more, then roll out the parantha into a 12.5cm/5 inch diameter.

4. Place carefully on a hot *tava*, allow the underneath side to cook for a minute. As soon as the bubbles appear turn it over, smear a teaspoon of ghee on this partly cooked side. Allow the underneath side to cook for a few seconds then turn it over.
5. Smear about a teaspoon of ghee on this side, also spread a little along the edges, so that it seeps on to the underneath side.
6. Repeat this, turning over and smearing ghee once more. This will really crisp up the parantha.
7. Remove from the *tava*, sprinkle a large pinch of dried mint on top and holding the parantha in both hands crumple it up into a ball. This will help to soften up the parantha yet keep its crispness. Serve immediately. This is one parantha that you just cannot stack up to be served later.

Serving suggestion
A delicious parantha to be served with an equally rich meat or poultry dish, a yogurt and a dal. Being extremely rich, it would be more than enough to serve 2 per person.

⊱•⊰

Nan

Anyone who is fond of Indian food has at some time or another tasted nan. Nan is one of the few varieties of Indian bread that is made with plain flour which is fermented with yeast or baking powder or soured yogurt or with a piece of dough that has been left for a day or two in a warm place. Once the dough has fermented, medium-sized pieces are broken off, slapped around between the palms of your hands in order to flatten and shape it into a round, then stuck on the side of a *tandoor*. The nan cooks within a few minutes, is removed with the help of two long metal skewers and eaten hot, as keeping nan for any length of time will only produce a cold, leathery, unappetizing bread. A fairly good substitute can be made in a conventional gas or electric oven, although it is the aroma of the clay and charcoal that enhances the flavour of nan.

Makes 10–12
Preparation time: 20 minutes plus 3–4 hours proving
Cooking time: 40 minutes

1 kg/2 lbs plain flour	1 egg
³/₄ teaspoon baking powder	100ml/4 fl.oz milk
¹/₄ teaspoon bicarbonate of soda	50ml/1 fl.oz water
	A little extra milk
Pinch of salt	25g/1 oz sesame seeds
1 teaspoon sugar	1 tablespoon nigella seeds

1. Place the flour, baking powder, bicarbonate of soda, salt and sugar in a bowl.
2. Break the egg into it and mix it thoroughly with your fingers.
3. Mix together the milk and the water. Pour a little of the mixture into the flour and knead it really hard to a soft smooth dough. (It is very important to knead it really well.)
4. Place the dough in a bowl, cover with polythene and leave to prove for 3–4 hours in a warm place (I find the airing cupboard the best place).
5. The dough should rise to twice its size.
6. Remove from the bowl, knead it well once again for 5–7 minutes and then divide it into 10–12 equal-sized portions.
7. Lightly grease two baking sheets. Preheat the oven to gas 7/220°C/425°F.
8. Roll out the dough into 12.5–15cm/5–6-inch rounds. Brush with a little milk, and sprinkle some sesame and nigella seeds on top.
9. Place on the baking sheets and bake in the preheated oven for 12–15 minutes. Serve hot.

Serve nan with a meat or poultry dish.

❦

Deep-fried Wholemeal Bread
Poori

With the exception of a few special Indian breads, most of them are made of wholemeal flour. Although made of the same dough as paranthas, pooris are heavier and richer because they are deep-fried in oil to a crisp golden colour. They should really be eaten immediately, but unfortunately that sort of a luxury can only be possible if there is another person in the kitchen frying these delicious concoctions.

Makes about 20
Preparation time: 15 minutes plus 15 minutes resting
Cooking time: 20–25 minutes

225g/8 oz wholemeal flour   Oil for deep-frying
1 dessertspoon oil
150ml/¹/₄ pint (approx.)
   water

1. Place the flour in a bowl, add the oil and mix it in with your fingers. Pour in a little water at a time to bind the flour into a stiffish dough. (Therefore a little less water than that mentioned might be used.) Cover with a damp cloth and leave to rest for about 15 minutes.
2. Heat some oil in a *karahi* or deep-fryer. (Drop a small piece of dough into the oil to test the heat. It should start frying at once and float to the top – if the oil is not hot enough then the poori will remain at the bottom and soak up excessive oil.)
3. Break off small pieces of the dough and shape into smooth

224

balls. Smear a little oil on the rolling surface to prevent the dough from sticking (if dry flour is used for this purpose then make sure that any excess flour is shaken off as that will burn in the hot oil).

4. Roll the ball of dough into a round of no more than 10cm/4 inches in diameter and very thin. Lift it off the rolling surface and slip it into the hot oil. (The best way to do this without splashing any oil on your hands is to hold the poori between your forefingers and thumbs, right next to the *karahi* or fryer, and gently let go. The poori will just slip into the hot fat.)

5. Using a perforated slice or spoon, gently keep pressing the poori into the oil, (it is best to press the edges first, then the centre). The poori will rise to the surface. After about half a minute turn the poori over and repeat the gentle pressing. This time the thin top layer will puff up like a balloon and prevent the poori from soaking up too much oil.

6. Lift the poori out with the slice or spoon, then hold it at an angle against the side of the pan for a few seconds to drain away any excess oil.

7. If possible serve at once; if not, then keep them wrapped up in a piece of foil.

Alternative suggestion

Like the paranthas, pooris can also be stuffed with various spicy mixtures, such as potatoes, ground moong dal, mince etc.

Desserts

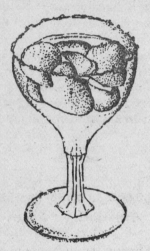

In a traditional Indian meal the dessert or pudding is very often served along with the savoury dishes, and left for the individual to eat whenever he or she wishes. Most traditional desserts are made of soft cheese – paneer – or from vegetables steeped in sugar syrup. These classic recipes are well documented and don't fit in with the concept of *New Indian Cookery* so I have omitted them.

Instead, I have devoted this chapter to new exciting recipes using combinations of the abundant tropical fruits which in the West seem exotic. Fruits such as apples, pears and grapes are considered a luxury in India, where they are available only in the short winter. Papaya, lychees, mangoes, custard apples, etc., which are run-of-the-mill fruits in tropical countries, are fortunately becoming readily available in the West. A classic dish such as *shrikand* has become the frozen yogurt flavoured with mango purée in this chapter. Paneer has been used as a base for mango cheesecake, an idea from the West. Mangoes, considered the king of fruits, are usually green, yellow or reddish with a luscious orangish pulp inside and a large stone. In this chapter recipes have been invented to include the pulp in a whole variety of ways.

Another fruit that is usually eaten as a savoury but has been used here as a dessert is avocado. Yogurt instead of cream has been used to create a lighter textured and more nutritious and slimming sauce. Bananas cooked in jaggery and butter are just the ultimate in taste. My purpose in creating exciting recipes with tropical fruits has been to introduce people in the West to the exotic fruits, and to encourage people in the East to treat them with a new awareness and respect.

◆◚◦◛◆

Frozen Guava Yogurt
Amrood ka Dahi

Various varieties of guava are available in India. Allahabad in central India is famous for its guavas, especially the light delicate pink ones. Although the outside skin is the characteristic yellow, the inside flesh is often a delicate pink. The seeds of guavas are hard, but delicious.

Serves 4–6
Preparation time: 30 minutes plus 3 hours freezing

600ml/1 pint homemade
   yogurt (page 47)
6 very ripe guavas with
   leaves
2 tablespoons icing sugar
25g/1 oz finely chopped
   blanched almonds

2 green cardamom pods
1 egg white, lightly beaten
2 tablespoons granulated
   sugar

1. Tie the yogurt in a piece of muslin and hang it up to drain for about 1 hour.
2. Chill in the refrigerator for 3–4 hours.
3. Peel the guavas and cut them into quarters. Carefully remove all the seeds. If any stalks and leaves are on the guavas, reserve them for decoration.
4. Place the deseeded guava quarters with the icing sugar in an electric blender or food processor and blend to a smooth paste.
5. Add the drained yogurt and blend for a further few minutes until smooth.
6. Lightly roast the almonds and depod the cardamoms. Crush the seeds to a fine powder.
7. Add the almonds and cardamom powder to the yogurt paste. Mix well.
8. Chill in the refrigerator for about 1 hour, then transfer into an ice-cream maker and freeze for about $1\frac{1}{2}$–2 hours.
9. The frozen yogurt is ready when the blades in the machine stop rotating.
10. Scoop out the yogurt and serve on individual plates.
11. Dip the fresh guava leaves first in the egg white and then in the granulated sugar. When dry, use to decorate the yogurt.

❦

Frozen Mango Yogurt
Aam ka Dahi

Frozen yogurts have recently become the in thing all over the West, and taken a very important place in the desserts of the world. Mango purée combined with natural homemade yogurt and frozen to the right consistency delicately complements a rich meal.

Serves 6–8
Preparation time: 20 minutes plus 3 hours freezing

1 litre/1³/₄ pints homemade   1 tablespoon rose water
  yogurt (page 000)   Icing sugar to taste
3 green cardamoms
450ml/15 fl.oz canned
  mango pulp

1. Drain the yogurt in a cheesecloth and leave it in the refrigerator overnight.
2. Beat the drained yogurt into a smooth paste.
3. Deskin the green cardamoms and crush. Mix together the mango pulp, rose water, cardamoms and icing sugar.
4. Add the mango pulp and beat thoroughly for about 5 minutes. The beating will smooth the mixture and incorporate enough air to make the mixture light and fluffy.
5. Pour the mixture into an ice-cream container, cover and place in the freezing compartment to chill. This will take about 1 hour.
6. Remove container from the freezer and place its contents in an ice-cream maker. Switch the machine on and place it back in the freezer.
7. The yogurt is ready for serving as soon as the machine stops. (This will take about 2 hours.) The consistency is rather soft so can be spooned out very easily.

Serving suggestion
Delicious and refreshing way to serve yogurt, especially after a rich meal.

Freezing hint
Although this will freeze very well, it will need to be thawed out partially before serving.

Saffron Yogurt
Kesar ka Meetha Dahi

Although a classic dish from the western region of India, I have gone a step further in making a superb dish more attractive and delicious. Saffron must be used with discretion, as too much of it can ruin the subtle taste and aroma of this delicate spice.

Serves 4–6
Preparation time: 30 minutes plus 2 hours chilling

1 litre/1³/₄ pints homemade yogurt (page 47)
2 tablespoons warm milk
Large pinch of saffron strands (about 10)

2–3 tablespoons granulated sugar
50g/2 oz unsalted pistachio nuts

1. Put the yogurt in a cheesecloth, tie up the ends and hang up to drain for about 2 hours.
2. Warm the milk, add the saffron and leave to infuse for 10 minutes.
3. Place the drained yogurt in a chilled bowl. Add the sugar and saffron milk. Stir well to blend into a smooth consistency and to dissolve the sugar.
4. Cut the pistachio nuts into halves lengthwise and mix half of them into the yogurt.
5. Transfer the yogurt into soufflé dishes. Cover with a large plate and chill in the refrigerator for at least 1–2 hours.
6. Decorate with the remaining pistachio halves just before serving.

Avocado Cream with Pistachio Nuts
Avocado Malai Piste Wali

Although avocadoes grow in large quantities in the south of India, they are virtually unknown in the north. Unlike in the West where avocadoes are eaten as a salad vegetable, the very ripe avocado in southern India is eaten as a fruit. It is with this feature in mind that I created this recipe. Yogurt can be replaced with either thick cream or custard base to make ice cream, but I find the tang of homemade yogurt enhances the bland flavour of the avocado.

Serves 4–6
Preparation time: 1¹/₂ hours plus 2 hours chilling

600 ml/1 pint homemade yogurt (page 47)
2–3 tablespoons caster sugar
2 very ripe avocadoes
1 tablespoon lemon juice
50g/2 oz unsalted pistachio nuts
50g/2 oz granulated sugar
Green colouring
1 egg white

1. Carefully drain the homemade yogurt in a cheesecloth or muslin and let it hang to drain for about 1 hour.
2. Place the drained yogurt in a blender or food processor along with the caster sugar.
3. Cut the avocadoes in half. Remove the stones and scoop out all the soft greeny-yellow flesh, place it into the blender or food processor along with the lemon juice.
4. Blend to a smooth consistency. Transfer into a bowl, cover and chill for 1¹/₂ hours.
5. Cut the pistachio nuts into slivers.
6. Next prepare 4–6 glass serving dishes. Place the granulated sugar in a saucer. Add 2–3 drops of green colouring. With a spoon mix the sugar to absorb the colour. The sugar will turn a delicate green colour.

7. Dip a pastry brush into the egg white and carefully brush it around the edge on the outside of each glass bowl.
8. Before the egg white has a chance to dry, hold each bowl upside down and dip into the coloured sugar. Slowly revolve the bowl, making sure that the coloured sugar sticks to the edges of the bowl.
9. Add half the slivered pistachio nuts to the avocado yogurt mixture and stir well.
10. Carefully spoon the mixture into the glass bowls taking care not to damage the sugared edges.
11. Decorate the avocado yogurt with the remaining pistachio nuts and serve really chilled.

⊷∘⊶

Mango Cheesecake
Aam aur Paneer ka Toffa

Cheesecake revolution swept the Western continent from America only a few years ago, so much so that cheesecakes have now become a part of our expanding food repertoire. I find the more exotic fruits like mango, nectarines, kiwi fruit, chikoo etc., introduce a new flavour and colour to the cheesecake. In this recipe I have used homemade paneer and natural yogurt on top of a digestive biscuit base.

Serves 6–8
Preparation time: 25–30 minutes plus 2 hours chilling
Cooking time: 30 minutes

450g/1 lb paneer (page 44)
300ml/¹/₂ pint natural yogurt (page 47)
225g/8 oz digestive biscuits
3 tablespoons melted butter

450ml/15 fl.oz can mango purée
2 heaped teaspoons arrowroot
1 tablespoon icing sugar

1. Make the paneer and the yogurt and drain them both (separately) for about half an hour.
2. Put the digestive biscuits into a food processor and crush finely. Transfer all but 2–3 tablespoons of the crumbs to a lightly buttered cake tin with a loose bottom. Using the back of your hand, firmly press down the crushed biscuit crumbs. Place in the freezer for about 20 minutes.
3. Empty the mango purée into a heavy-based saucepan. Mix the arrowroot with a little of the purée and about 1 tablespoon of water to produce a smooth consistency.
4. Add this to the mango purée and, stirring continuously, bring it to the boil. At once reduce the heat and, stirring continuously, keep simmering for a few minutes until the purée thickens.
5. Remove from the heat, cover and cool by covering the pan and standing it in ice-cold water (if left uncovered, a thick skin will form and ruin the purée).
6. Place the drained paneer in the food processor and switch on for a few seconds to break it down into a smooth paste.
7. Sieve the icing sugar into the food processor and add the drained yogurt. Switch on for a minute to blend the cheese and yogurt to a smooth consistency.
8. Remove the cake tin from the freezer and top it up with the cheese and yogurt mixture. Smooth it down, especially around the edges. Return it to the freezer for another 20 minutes.
9. By this time the mango purée should be absolutely cold. Carefully pour it over the cheese base.
10. Place the filled cake tin in the refrigerator for about $1\frac{1}{2}$ hours to chill it thoroughly.
11. Carefully slice a knife around the edges of the cake tin and gently prise the loose bottom away from the tin to a flat surface.
12. Using two large, flat fish slices, carefully slide the cheesecake off the cake tin base and on to a serving dish.

13. Sprinkle the remaining biscuit crumbs all around the edges and serve at room temperature.

✐◦✎

Mango Boats
Aam ki Kishtiya

Mango, the king of fruit, unfortunately has a very short season in India, but we here in the United Kingdom are indeed very lucky as mangoes from different parts of the world are available in most supermarkets all the year round. Mangoes are best served chilled either on their own, or with fresh cream or yogurt sauce.

Serves 4
Preparation time: 30 minutes plus 2 hours chilling

300ml/½ pint natural yogurt (page 47)
2 teaspoons aniseeds, lightly crushed

1 tablespoon icing sugar, sieved
4 ripe but firm mangoes
50g/2 oz slivered almonds

1. Tie the yogurt into a cheesecloth or muslin and hang for half an hour to drain.
2. Place the drained yogurt into a small bowl and add the aniseeds and icing sugar. Mix well to a smooth consistency. Chill for 2 hours in the refrigerator. (The yogurt will thicken slightly by then.)
3. Using a very sharp knife, cut each mango into two large pieces, one either side of its large stone. Then, using the sharp point of the knife, cut through the flesh to form cubes, being careful not to cut through the skin.
4. Lightly roast the slivered almonds. Allow to cool.
5. Place 2 mango pieces on each plate. Carefully pour over

the chilled yogurt sauce and decorate with the slivered almonds.
6. Serve well chilled.

Sweet Mango Fritters
Aam ke Meethe Pakore

Although mangoes eaten in their natural state are a delicacy in their own right, I find a coating of crisp batter turns them into something special. These can then be flamed in the true French style or served with whipped cream.

Serves 4
Preparation time: 20 minutes
Cooking time: 20 minutes

4 large ripe mangoes
Oil for deep-frying
25g/1 oz chopped almonds
100g/4 oz whipped cream

Batter
100g/4 oz plain flour
1 tablespoon lightly crushed aniseeds
150ml/5 fl.oz milk
1 large egg white

1. Carefully peel the mangoes. From each one, cut off two large slices, one from each side of the stone.
2. Prepare the batter by beating together the plain flour, aniseeds and milk until really smooth.
3. Whip the egg white until stiff and gently fold it into the batter.
4. Heat the oil in a deep-fat fryer or *karahi*.

235

5. Dip the mango slices into the batter and carefully immerse each one in the hot fat. Fry, turning once, to a rich golden colour.
6. Drain, sprinkle a few almonds on top and serve at once with whipped cream.

⟐⟐⟐

Guava Baskets Tani
Amrood ki Tokariya Tani

A delicious and lightly perfumed fruit which contains about ten times as much vitamin C as an orange. It grows in most tropical and subtropical countries. As the fruit ripens and then goes bad very quickly, it is best to eat it soon after purchase. If fresh guavas are not available, then the canned ones are not a bad substitute.

Serves 4
Preparation time: 20 minutes
Cooking time: 5 minutes

4 large ripe guavas
25g/1 oz chopped almonds
Seeds of 2 green cardamoms

150ml/5 fl.oz double cream
1 tablespoon clear honey

1. Carefully peel the guavas, using either a sharp knife or a potato peeler.
2. To make the baskets, first hold the peeled guava firmly. With the tip of a sharp knife mark a line halfway down and around the guava, leaving a gap of about 1cm/^{1}/$_2$ inch approximately at midway. Make an incision towards the top along this width to form the handle. Thus you have divided the guava into half for the bottom basket and into 2 quarters, leaving a handle of 1cm/^{1}/$_2$ inch at the top half.
3. Carefully cut out the quarters to leave a basket shape.

4. Again using the sharp knife, carefully cut out the seeds and discard them. You will now be left with a hollow guava shell and handle. Chill in the fridge.
5. Lightly toast the almonds to a pale golden colour. Crush the cardamoms to a fine powder.
6. Whip the double cream to a stiffish consistency, add the almonds and cardamoms and mix well.
7. Pour in the honey and quickly fold it in with a metal spoon. (Be careful not to overwhip the cream as it will start to separate.)
8. Spoon this cream and honey mixture into the guava baskets right up to the brim. They should look full.
9. Serve really well chilled.

❧❦

Fresh Fruit Salad with Yogurt Sauce
Taje Phalon ka Salat

A refreshing hot dessert where natural yogurt has been used as a topping rather than fresh double cream. I find cinnamon powder enhances the tangy taste of the yogurt and complements the fresh fruit. To make it something special I would advise you to flambé it with your best cognac, be it Rémy Martin or Courvoisier.

Serves 4
Preparation time: 25 minutes
Cooking time: 10 minutes

1 ripe banana
2 ripe peaches
2 slices pineapple
1 crisp apple
Small bunch of grapes
200ml/6 fl.oz natural yogurt
2 teaspoons cornflour

1/2 teaspoon cinnamon
   powder
1/4 teaspoon nutmeg
2 tablespoons dark brown
   sugar
2 tablespoons brandy

1. Although I have mentioned a selection of fruit, the choice is entirely yours. Peel the appropriate fruit and either slice it or cut into chunks. Transfer to an ovenproof dish.
2. Lightly beat the yogurt, add the cornflour and mix it in thoroughly. No cornflour lumps should remain.
3. Transfer the yogurt to a small, heavy-bottomed saucepan, place over low heat and, stirring continously, thicken the yogurt sauce.
4. As soon as it starts bubbling, remove from the heat but continue stirring. (The cornflour will prevent the yogurt from curdling.)
5. Pour the yogurt sauce over the fruit salad.
6. Sprinkle the cinnamon, nutmeg and brown sugar on top. Place under a hot grill until the sugar starts to melt and bubble.
7. Heat the brandy in a small pan and flambé it. Pour the flambé over the yogurt sauce and serve at once.

◆━◦━◆

Pears in Rooh Afza
Nashpati Rooh Afza

Wine-making being a very young industry in India, Indian wines leave a lot to be desired. And as the majority of Indians are non-alcoholic drinkers, the choice in wines is very limited. Rooh afza is a concentrated syrup readily available and forms the basis of a refreshing cold drink. I have used this diluted syrup to make a variation of the classical French dish, pears in red wine.

Serves 4
Preparation time: 20 minutes
Cooking time: 35–40 minutes

150ml/¼ pint rooh afza syrup
300ml/½ pint cold water
Small stick of cinnamon
4 ripe pears (preferably the same size)

2 teaspoons arrowroot
50g/2 oz flaked almonds
150ml/¼ pint double cream

1. Dilute the syrup with the water, add the cinnamon stick and gently bring to the boil. Reduce the heat and simmer.
2. Carefully peel the pears, keeping the stalks intact. Cut off a piece at the other end so that the pears stand straight.
3. Stand the pears in the simmering syrup. Cover with a lid and leave to cook gently for about 30–35 minutes until the pears are really tender and have absorbed some of the syrup.
4. Using a slotted spoon, carefully remove the cooked pears and put them in a glass serving bowl.
5. Dilute the arrowroot in a little water and add it to the simmering syrup. Stirring constantly, allow the sauce to boil and thicken.
6. Pour the thickened sauce over all the cooked pears.
7. Lightly toast the almond flakes under a hot grill for a few minutes, turning them frequently.
8. Allow to cool enough to handle. Carefully stick some toasted almonds to the pears, thus giving them a flecked appearance.
9. Place the bowl in the fridge to chill completely before serving.
10. Whip the double cream to the right consistency and serve with the pears.

Gambles Banana Jaggery
Gambles Gurd ke Kayle

Jaggery has its own taste and texture, quite distinct from refined brown sugar. This dish was created one night in Sri Lanka when we were having a barbecue on the beach. I barbecued the small ripe bananas in their skins then peeled them and sautéd them in a delicious sauce of jaggery and butter, and flambéd with Courvoisier – the only cognac we possessed.

Serves 4
Preparation time: 10 minutes
Cooking time: 20 minutes

4 very ripe small bananas
50–75g/2–3 oz butter
100g/4 oz jaggery, coarsely
  grated

2 tablespoons cognac or
  brandy

1. If a barbecue is already hot, place unpeeled bananas on the grill and barbecue for 15 minutes. If you don't have a barbecue, place the unpeeled bananas under the grill for 10 minutes, turning once or twice.
2. Melt the butter in a frying pan, add the grated jaggery and, stirring continuously to prevent it sticking, let it melt.
3. Peel the bananas and, if large, cut into half lengthwise. Carefully immerse them in the jaggery sauce and let them cook for a few minutes. Turn them over once very carefully as they break easily.
4. Transfer to serving dishes and spoon the sauce over the bananas.
5. Heat the cognac and set light to it. At once pour it over the bananas.

Steamed Yogurt Windsor Manor
Dum ka Dahi Windsor Manor

My last visit to India was specially made to organize the final details of a proposed gourmet tour that I am taking to various parts of the country. I stayed at some of the best hotels the vast country has to offer, including Windsor Manor in Bangalore. Chef Chakrabarti there created for me this delicious yogurt dish, which the gourmet tour guests will also taste.

Serves 4–6
Preparation time: 30 minutes
Cooking time: 1½ hours

600ml/1 pint homemade
    yogurt (page 47)
A few strands of saffron
1 tablespoon milk

450ml/15 fl.oz can
    condensed milk
Seeds of 4 green cardamoms,
    lightly crushed

For decoration
25g/1 oz unsalted pistachio
    nuts, finely sliced, *or* a
    small bunch of grapes, 1
    egg white and 1
    tablespoon caster sugar
    (see below)

1. Carefully tie up the yogurt in cheesecloth or muslin and hang up to drain for about half an hour.
2. Warm the milk, add the saffron. Leave to infuse for 10 minutes.
3. Empty the can of condensed milk into a bowl. Add the drained yogurt, cardamom seeds, and the saffron-flavoured milk.
4. Using a whisk, whip the mixture to a smooth, fairly thick

241

consistency. Pour into a fluted mould and cover with greaseproof paper.

5. Prepare a steamer and place the fluted mould inside it, making sure that the water is just simmering and not touching the mould.

6. Cover with the lid and allow to steam for about $1^{1}/_{2}$ hours. (Add boiling water to the steamer if required.)

7. Remove the greaseproof paper and feel the steamed pudding. It should feel firm to the touch and come away from the edges when pulled.

8. Remove from the steamer. Place the mould upside down on to a serving dish. Holding it firmly with both hands, give a mighty shake and the pudding should come away clean from the mould. (I usually keep my fingers crossed.)

9. The beauty of this pudding is that it can be served hot or cold. If serving cold, chill the pudding for at least 1 hour then decorate with frosted grapes: brush the grapes with egg white, sprinkle with sugar and refrigerate until set hard. If serving hot, decorate with pistachio slivers.

Sweet Saffron Rice
Meethe Kesar ke Chawal

A classic dish which is cooked on special occasions. The delicate yellow colour and the subtle aroma of saffron is something quite exquisite. Turmeric should never be used instead of saffron, even though saffron is the most expensive spice in the world whereas turmeric is the cheapest.

Serves 4
Preparation time: 10 minutes plus 30 minutes soaking
Cooking time: 30 minutes

175g/6 oz basmati rice
2 tablespoons milk
Small pinch of saffron
  strands
2 tablespoons ghee
2 cloves
50g/2 oz green raisins,
  washed and drained
50g/2 oz slivered almonds

Seeds of 2 green cardamoms,
  lightly crushed
1 tablespoon clear honey
Enough water to reach
  2.5cm/1 inch above the
  rice
Silver paper (optional)
150ml/$^1/_4$ pint single cream

1. Thoroughly wash the rice and soak it for about 30 minutes. Drain carefully and keep aside.
2. Warm up the milk in a small pan, add saffron strands and leave to infuse for about 10 minutes. (Good saffron will infuse very rapidly and release its colour.)
3. Meanwhile heat the ghee, then add the cloves, green raisins, slivered almonds and cardamom seeds. Stir-fry for a couple of minutes until the almonds start to turn a pale golden colour.
4. Add the rice and stir well for another few seconds.
5. Dilute the honey with the saffron milk and pour it into the rice. Stir well then level the rice.
6. Pour in the water.
7. Stir gently to mix the ingredients, then reduce the heat, cover with a tight-fitting lid and leave to cook for about 20 minutes. It is important that the lid is not removed during this time.
8. Gently fluff up the rice with a fork and transfer it to a fluted ring mould. Press down gently, and carefully invert the mould on to a serving dish.
9. Decorate with silver paper if available and serve with slightly chilled fresh cream.

Soft Cheese Pudding
Paneer ke Kheer

Rabri, a traditional dish made all over India, requires a lot of time and patience in preparing. Crumbled paneer makes an excellent substitute when mixed with evaporated milk. An instant dessert.

Serves 4–6
Preparation time: 30 minutes plus 1 hour chilling
Cooking time: 10 minutes

100g/4oz paneer (page 44)
450ml/15 fl.oz can
  evaporated milk
1¹/₂ tablespoons icing sugar
25g/1 oz slivered almonds
25g/1 oz slivered unsalted
  pistachio nuts

25g/1 oz green raisins,
  washed
Seeds of 2 green cardamoms,
  lightly crushed
1 teaspoon rose water
Silver paper (optional)

1. Prepare the paneer, hang it up to drain for 10 minutes, then rinse it under a cold tap. Keep crumbling the cheese with your fingers to break up the granules.
2. Hang up to drain for about 15 minutes. In the meantime empty the evaporated milk into a bowl, sieve the icing sugar into it and beat lightly with a fork to mix.
4. Add the slivered almonds, pistachio nuts, raisins, cardamom seeds and rose water. Stir well for a few seconds, then add the crumbled paneer.
5. Whisk lightly with a fork to mix in the paneer. Place the bowl in the refrigerator and chill thoroughly before serving.
6. Decorate with silver paper just before serving.

Lychees with Crystallized Ginger
Lychees aur Meetha Adrak

Although fresh lychees in the West are expensive, they are worth every penny. It is a truly delicious fruit which has a dark pink knobbly skin which, when peeled, reveals an almost transparent whitish pulp with one or two large black seeds. The delicate perfume of this luscious fruit reminds me of fragrant roses on a hot summer's day. As fresh lychees, apart from being expensive, are quite difficult to come by, for this recipe I have used canned lychees, which although can't match the fresh ones are not a bad replacement. The delicate taste of the lychees is further enhanced by the addition of the sharp spicy taste of crystallized ginger.

Serves 4
Preparation time: 10 minutes plus 2 hours chilling

50g/2 oz sugar
A few drops of red food
  colouring

1 egg white
25g/1 oz crystallized ginger
1 large can lychees

1. Put the sugar in a saucer and add the food colouring. Mix well to turn the sugar to a deep pink colour.
2. Dip a pastry brush in the egg white and carefully brush it all around the edge of 4 glass bowls. Hold each bowl upside down and dip it into the coloured sugar. The sugar will stick to the egg white. Leave to set.
3. Finely slice the ginger into thin slivers.
4. Turn out the lychees into a bowl, add the ginger slivers and mix well.
5. Carefully transfer the lychees into the glass bowls without disturbing the crystallized edges.
6. Chill well before serving.

Serving suggestion

A delicious dessert to follow a fairly large and rich meal, to balance the guilt of overindulgence. The delicate taste tends to linger in the mouth for quite a long time.

Chutneys and Drinks

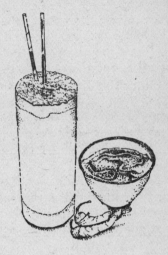

Chutneys and spicy drinks are second nature to most Indians, so you may well ask what is so different about the chutneys and drinks described here. The answer is that the handful of chutneys and drinks in this chapter differs from their traditional counterparts in the combination of ingredients. A chutney made of natural yogurt with freshly chopped dill to be served with fish is delicious and refreshing.

The chutneys in this chapter can be used as stuffings for meat, poultry and vegetables as well as to accompany main dishes. The spicy mint chutney, although quite common, forms a delicious stuffing for a leg of lamb which is then roasted in the oven or over a barbecue. This chutney not only adds zing to the meat but looks most attractive when the meat is carved. The coconut chutney forms a unique and different stuffing for boiled cauliflower, which is smothered in spices and baked in an oven. The instant yogurt and mint chutney, when made in large quantity, is an excellent and refreshing salad dressing for boiled potatoes or crunchy celery and apples.

These chutneys, however they are used, liven up any meal, whether plain or rich.

Most soft fruits, such as papaya, mangoes, apricots and dates, to name a few, make excellent chutneys. As there are various types of chutney they are best divided into two categories: the cooked and the uncooked. The cooked variety, of course, takes longer to prepare but can also be stored for a length of time in a cool dry place. The uncooked variety is easy and quick to prepare and best kept for no more than a week. The important fact to remember when making chutneys is that the minimum amount of water should be used, as that is what 'spoils' the chutney.

Delicious sweet, spicy, or tangy chutneys should not be reserved just for the main meal. A thin layer spread on brown bread or crispbread transforms the plain bread into a most appetizing snack, good enough to be shared with friends.

As soon as anyone mentions tea, people immediately think of India, the world's largest producer of a wide variety of teas growing in the Himalayan foothills in the north east and the Nilgiri Mountains in the south. Although the tea plants grew wild in Assam, they were only discovered in 1823 and it wasn't until much later that tea plants were cultivated on a large scale. My father recalls his young days when free tea stalls were set up along the Indian roadsides in an effort to promote tea. Such drastic marketing efforts are no longer needed for tea. Today each country has its own recipes for making the best cup of tea. Some people like to add hot milk, others cold. Some advocate that milk should be poured first, others hold the reverse opinion. Indians, on the other hand, prefer to boil the tea leaves along with the milk, sugar and a few choice spices such as cinnamon, cardamoms, black pepper, cloves, aniseed and even almonds. Whatever the spice addition, it creates the most refreshing drink. In this chapter, I have included just one such recipe for spiced tea. Not only is this tea delicious but it also acts as a medicine to cure minor ailments such as colds and coughs.

But apart from tea, other cool refreshing drinks are a necessity in the hot climate of India. The delicious fresh lime drinks fall in a category of their own. I find that lime juice has more tang and flavour than lemon, although the one can be substituted for the other if necessary. *Nimboo pani* – lime water – is a common drink during the hot summer months. Some like it salty and others like it sweet; some dilute it with water, others with soda; some like it plain, others with ground spices sprinkled on top. The lime drink in this chapter is truly mouthwatering as a few drops of Worcestershire and tabasco sauce increase the flavour and add just the right amount of kick to the drink. There is nothing to stop you adding some gin or vodka or any other spirit to this delicious concoction. The same could be said for the fresh ginger drink, which can be made up into a concentrate and diluted with water or soda.

Lassi – thin yogurt drink – must rank among the most popular and widely drunk mixes throughout India, and it is also catching on in the West. As well as being healthy, it reduces the hunger pangs as it is very filling. For this reason it is excellent for people counting their calories. To the lassi in this chapter I have added some freshly squeezed ginger juice, then thoroughly chilled it before serving. A drink to remember.

Coconut Chutney
Nariyal ki Chutney

Coconut chutney is a delight, especially to people who normally don't use coconut in their cooking. If freshly grated coconut is not available then use the desiccated variety.

2 green chillies	1 tablespoon lemon juice
4 tablespoons natural yogurt	1 teaspoon salt
50g/2 oz freshly grated coconut	

Finely grind the green chillies, lightly beat the yogurt, mix all the ingredients together and keep in a cool place until needed.

Fresh Ginger and Lime Chutney
Adrak aur Nimboo ki Chutney

This delicious combination of fresh ginger, lime juice, green chillies and black pepper has proved a great success with everyone who has tried it.

100g/4 oz fresh ginger	1¼ teaspoons salt
25g/1 oz green chillies	2 teaspoons sugar
4 tablespoons lime juice	
1 teaspoon coarsely ground black pepper	

1. Peel and coarsely grate the ginger. Reserve any juice.

2. Remove the chillies' stalks and shred the chillies into very thin long strips.
3. Mix all the ingredients including the ginger juice and stir well to dissolve the salt and sugar.
4. Store in a glass gar for a couple of days to mature.

Green Chilli Chutney
Hari Mirch ki Chutney

Chutneys and pickles form a very important part of the Indian meal. A hot spicy chutney really whets the appetite. Green chillies can vary in their fiery strength from one chilli to another, so if the first chutney turned out too mild don't take it for granted that every one will be the same. Keeps well for a few weeks in the fridge.

50g/2 oz fresh firm green chillies
1 large onion
Small bunch of coriander leaves

2 tablespoons lemon juice
1 teaspoon salt

1. Wash the chillies and cut off their stalks.
2. Peel and coarsely slice the onion.
3. Carefully wash the coriander leaves and shake them dry.
4. Place all the ingredients in a blender or food processor and grind to a smooth paste.

Mint and Green Chilli Chutney
Podine aur Hari Mirch ki Chutney

A chutney that can be used with leg of lamb. Its consistency is slightly grainy as the pomegranate seeds will not grind to a fine texture, but this gives the chutney a bit of bite. It can be made in advance and stored in a cool place.

100g/4 oz fresh mint leaves
1 large onion
2 tablespoons dried
   pomegranate seeds
2–3 green chillies

1–2 unripe green mangoes
1 teaspoon sugar
1–2 tablespoons water
1 teaspoon salt

1. Thoroughly wash the mint leaves and shake them dry.
2. Peel and chop the onion.
3. Wash the pomegranate seeds in a few changes of water. Leave to soak in a bowl for a few minutes.
4. Cut off the chilli stalks.
5. Peel the mangoes and cut them into chunks. Discard the seeds.
6. Scoop out the pomegranate seeds being careful not to disturb the sediment.
7. Place all the ingredients in a liquidizer or food processor and blend to a smooth purée. Use as required.

Mint and Yogurt Chutney
Dahi aur Podine ki Chutney

A delicious chutney that can be prepared right at the last minute and served with a large variety of snacks such as kebabs and grilled fish.

| 2 tablespoons natural yogurt | ½ teaspoon chilli powder |
| 1 teaspoon dried mint | ½ teaspoon salt |

Lightly beat the yogurt, mix in all the other ingredients and chill for a few minutes before serving.

＊

Mixed Chutney
Milihui Chutney

A unique combination of two strong-flavoured herbs – coriander leaves and mint leaves – with tamarind juice giving it added tang. A quick and easy chutney to make.

50g/2 oz coriander leaves	3 green chillies
75g/3 oz mint leaves	1 teaspoon ground cumin
2.5cm/1-inch piece of fresh	1 teaspoon salt
ginger	4 tablespoons tamarind juice
1 large onion	(page 50)

1. Thoroughly wash the coriander and mint leaves and shake them dry.
2. Peel and chop the ginger and onion. Remove the chilli stalks.
3. Place all the ingredients in a blender or food processor and grind to a smooth paste.

Yogurt Dill Chutney

3 tablespoons natural yogurt
Small bunch of fresh dill
1cm/^{1}/$_2$-inch piece of fresh
  ginger

^{1}/$_2$ teaspoon salt
Freshly ground black pepper

Lightly beat the yogurt in a bowl. Finely chop the dill and peel and finely shred the ginger. Mix together all the ingredients just before serving. (It is important that salt is added at the last minute as it tends to make the yogurt very watery.)

━━●●━━

Cinnamon and Cardamon Tea
Dalchini Illaichi ki Chai

One thing that the British left behind in India is tea, which before they arrived was an unknown plant in that vast country. Tea, apart from being a refreshing drink during the hot summer months and a warming one during winter, is also brewed with various herbs and spices to cure minor ailments such as colds, coughs etc. This style of tea has to be brewed, or rather boiled, along with the spice to get the maximum benefit.

Makes 600ml/1 pint

600ml/1 pint water
3 green cardamoms
Small stick of cinnamon

^{1}/$_2$ teaspoon aniseeds
1^1/$_2$ teaspoons tea leaves
Milk and sugar to taste

1. Combine all the ingredients – except the milk and sugar – in a saucepan, bring to the boil, then allow to simmer gently for 5–7 minutes so that all the goodness from the spices is extracted.

2. Add the required amount of milk and simmer for another minute.
3. Strain straight into cups, add sugar if used, and serve hot.

Cinnamon and Ginger Drink
Dalchini aur Adrak a Nasha

One day I was trying out some recipes for stocks using a wide variety of spices, and in a pan I had boiled some cinnamon, ginger and aniseed. On tasting it, I found it to be too delicious to use just as a stock, so added some sugar and turned it into a cold drink. As this became a success with my friends, I constantly experimented with different kinds of sugar. The best flavour came into existence when I added some jaggery. Its lovely musky smell and taste combines well with cinnamon and ginger.

Makes about 1¼ litres /2¼ pints

5cm/2-inch piece of fresh
  ginger
1 litre/1¾ pints water
5cm/2-inch stick of
  cinnamon

1 teaspoon aniseeds
225g/8 oz jaggery

1. Peel and lightly crush the ginger.
2. Place the water, ginger, cinnamon and aniseeds in a pan, bring to the boil then gently simmer for about 15 minutes.
3. Strain and allow to cool.
4. Add the jaggery and dissolve it completely.
5. Chill well before serving.

Ginger Lassi
Adrak ki Lassi

The most common drink made with natural yogurt is lassi. Natural yogurt is thinned a little with water and served either sweet or savoury. A truly refreshing drink during the hot summer months.

Serves 4
Preparation time: 10 minutes

300ml/^{1}/$_2$ pint natural yogurt
750ml/1^1/$_4$ pints cold water
2 tablespoons fresh ginger
  juice

1 teaspoon salt
Dash of freshly milled black
  pepper
Plenty of crushed ice

1. Place all the ingredients except the ice in a liquidizer and mix together at high speed.
2. Divide the crushed ice into 4 portions, so that it half-fills the tall glasses.
3. Pour the cold lassi into tall glasses and serve at once.

Note: As fresh ginger juice is not available it has to be prepared at home. Scrape off the thin skin. Cut the ginger into small pieces. Place in a liquidizer or herb chopper and mince finely. Then squeeze the pulp either using your hand or with a large ginger-squeezer.

Serving suggestion
Serve chilled either as part of the meal or as an appetizer before the meal.

Freezing hint
Ginger juice freezes well. Freeze in an ice-cube tray. Once frozen, transfer to a polythene bag and store. Can be used in other dishes that require fresh ginger.

⊱•⊰

Fresh Lime Water
Nimboo ka Pani

There is nothing quite so refreshing as freshly squeezed lime juice, whether it is used in a salad or diluted to make a delicious drink. I seem to exist on this when in India, as it rejuvenates every part of the body and is a tremendous source of vitamin C.

Makes 600ml/1 pint

600ml/1 pint ice cold-water
1 teaspoon salt
Dash of tabasco sauce
Dash of Worcestershire
  sauce

2–3 ripe yellow or green
  limes
Lots of crushed ice
A few thin slices of lime to
  decorate

1. Pour the water, salt, tabasco and Worcestershire sauce into a glass jug.
2. Squeeze the juice from the limes, strain and add to the water. Stir well to mix all the ingredients.
3. Place lots of crushed ice in each glass. Pour the ice-cold lime water on top, decorate with the slices of lime and serve.

Index

259

261

263

265

271